Published by Arva Parks & Company, P.O. Box 145358, Coral Gables, Fla. 33114-5358 in conjunction with Lion & Thorne Publishing, Tulsa, Oklahoma

ISBN 0-914381-04-0

The Florida Hurricane & Disaster

1 9 2 6

L.F. Reardon

Introduction by Arva Moore Parks

Remembrance of Hurricanes Past

Chicago had its fire.
San Francisco had its earthquake.
South Florida had its hurricane.

There was only one real hurricane. When South Floridians speak of "the hurricane," everyone knows which storm is meant — the infamous storm of 1926. Hurricanes had no official names then, and so it became known simply as the killer hurricane of 1926.

The 1926 hurricane has become a benchmark in South Florida history, a dividing point in time, much like B.C. and A.D. It has achieved a mystique of almost biblical proportions — akin to Noah's flood or the destruction of Sodom and Gomorrah.

When I was a little girl, it seemed like hurricanes came around every year, much like Christmas and my birthday. My father took them very seriously. As soon as he heard or read the word 'hurricane,' he set out the hurricane map and began tracking the storm. Grady Norton, the U.S. Weather Bureau hurricane expert, became part of our lives in those times. I can still hear his soft southern accented voice coming over the radio as "Mr. Hurricane" reported from the top floor of old Tech High (until recently the home of Dade County Public School administration).

Everyone in my family knew that if "Mr. Hurricane" posted hurricane warnings, my father would metamorphose from a weatherman to a top sergeant, galvanizing his wife and three children into a well-trained platoon of storm troopers.

My brother — cursing the fact that he had two sisters — got the worst of the duties. He had to help my father get out the heavy wooden storm shutters and board up every window and door.

As the youngest in the family, I usually accompanied my mother to the store to buy nonperishable food, cans of Sterno, candles and a jug of kerosene. We bought what seemed to be enough unappetizing canned goods to last a year. Fortunately for us kids, Mother always purchased what we called our "Hurricane Hershey Bars." To this day, I cannot eat a Hershey bar (or a Vienna sausage) without thinking about hurricanes.

By this time, the wind would be picking up a little as intermittent squalls with their ominous black clouds passed through. In between the showers, the sun usually reappeared. By the time we got home, the shutters were in place and the house was dark and stuffy. My sister and I were put to work cleaning the hurricane lamps which had been sitting on a high shelf since the last hurricane scare. We filled the bathtub and every pot and pan in the house with water — just in case the city water was shut off or polluted by the storm.

As the storm grew nearer, the wind began to whine and whistle through the cracks of the shutters. Then the rains came — pounding as the wind mixed with the deluge. Inevitably, the lights went out and so did the telephone. We sat huddled together in one room, listening to the eerie sounds of fury about us, heightened by the shadows from the flickering hurricane lamp.

My father never slept during a storm. Well supplied with newspapers and towels, he kept up a constant patrol, flashlight in hand, drying and damming up water that always leaked through somewhere.

Before we had a battery-powered radio, he became the forecaster, keeping his eye on the barometer, recording every drop in pressure. He also monitored the direction of the wind, always keeping a leeward door open so the decreasing pressure would not create a vacuum and blow the roof off our buttoned-up house.

If the storm hit us directly and we experienced a lull as the eye of the storm passed over, my father allowed us to go outside for a few minutes. He first checked for fallen wires, and we had to promise to stay in the yard. We were well trained in hurricanes, so as soon as the wind began to pick up from the opposite direction, we headed back in. Once in a while, there was an overwhelming urge to lean into the wind just one more

ii

time. But we usually scurried back into the house through the one open door that he quickly nailed shut. Then he opened another door on the opposite side of the house to adjust the house pressure much like my mother did her pressure cooker.

The aftermath was another story. The yard was usually a total disaster. Everyone had to help clean up; but my brother was again stuck with the worst of it. He once counted more than a thousand pieces of fruit — grapefruit, avocadoes, oranges, lemons and guavas — as we piled it up. The electric power and the telephone were usually off for days afterwards. (In 1950, the electricity was off three weeks.) By the time, it came back on, it seemed like pure heaven.

My serious and cautious father — who usually followed the hurricane rules to the letter of the law — bent only one. He was a very curious man; and even though everyone was admonished not to go sightseeing, we always piled into our Hudson for the grand tour to see what God had wrought. He rationalized our tour as an educational experience — and indeed it was. He always pointed out situations which could have been avoided if the people had taken the hurricane seriously and prepared for it.

The Baker's Haulover bridge was always on our tour route. Until the present bridge was built, the angry ocean severed the bridge from shore during every hurricane that I can remember. There were other areas of hurricane damage that were always predictable. The bayfront always looked like an outdoor boat show with boats tossed every-which-way by the storm tide. And most of the time, Hialeah was flooded as the Everglades rose up to reclaim the land.

The 1926 storm left the center section of the Baker's Haulover Bridge standing alone in the middle of the cut. *Miami News.*

Downed power lines and debris surrounded Rooney Plaza Hotel as the storm raged through the city. The photo was one of the first to come out of Miami. The original description sent along with the photograph described Miami as being "visited by a tornado which did millions of dollars damage as well as taking many lives in toll." *Miami News.*

For all my early hurricane experience, I have only been through two storms as an adult — Cleo and Betsy. Only one of these was as a home owner. I learned my father's lessons well and boarded up for hurricane David. Even though it did not hit us, I know that I did the right thing. Under the same circumstances, I would do the same thing again. I will never underestimate the power or unpredictability of a hurricane. I will never take it lightly. I fear my father would roll over in his grave if I ever attended a 'hurricane party.' My children, on the other hand, have never been in a hurricane.

A Frightening Surprise

I thought, with all this background, I knew a lot about hurricanes. I have pictured myself as sort of a native expert, having been through those storms with my father. As a historian and native Miamian, I have continued to be fascinated with the 1926 hurricane. I have heard stories about it all my life. But as I began researching in earnest, looking back at the contemporary newspaper accounts, talking to survivors, looking for pictures,

I came to the conclusion that here was an important story — and one with a timely parallel.

As I talked to those who had been here those fateful 12 hours that changed the course of Miami's history, I always asked them — was it our worst hurricane because people were unprepared for it — or because it was actually more severe? The answer was always the same: it was a deadly combination: it was our worst hurricane because people were unprepared and because it was more severe.

Actually, the storm was a frightening surprise. There were no sophisticated warning systems in the old days. The U.S. Weather Bureau in Miami knew it was out there brewing in the Caribbean. It had noted three storms in the newspapers as early as September 15. But the story had been buried on the back pages. On September 16, the *Miami Daily News* reported the whereabouts of the three storms on page 17 but added that the intensity of the third storm (the one which would hit) was not known.

September 17 was a beautiful day. The sun was bright, and a light breeze blew. On the morning of September 17, the *Miami Herald* carried a four-inch story on page one under the heading

At the Roman Pools along Miami Beach, trees bent double. The windmill in the center of the photograph was later torn down. *Miami News.*

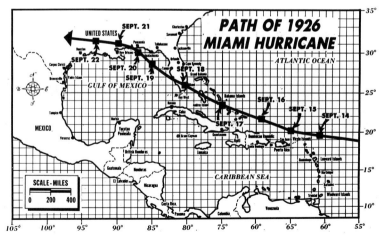

Path of 1926 Miami Hurricane. *Miami News.*

"Hurricane Reported." But the editors added that it was not expected to hit Florida. South Florida's 300,000 people went about their daily activities unconcerned. Most of the people had never been in a major hurricane even though they thought they had. A minor hurricane had grazed Miami only two months before; but it caused little damage. Coconut Grove pioneer Ralph M. Munroe hoped that it would "put the fear of the Lord into the scoffers." It had the opposite effect; people decided that a hurricane was just a bad storm — a nuisance to be endured.

When the *Miami Daily News* came out that afternoon, September 17, the page one lead story headline read: "Miami Warned of Tropical Storm." A subhead read "Disturbance is Headed for Nassau, Weather Bureau Advises." The *News* also reported that Weather Chief Richard W. Gray had hoisted northeast storm warnings (gale warnings) about noon and had warned of "destructive winds" in the late evening-early morning hours. The stories seemed hardly to be warnings. No one used the word hurricane, and few paid any attention.

By the late hours of September 17, when the winds began to build, people realized that a storm was upon them. Richard Gray holed up in his office in what is now the Amerifirst Building on N.E. First Street and First Avenue, watching the pressure fall. It dropped so rapidly that the barograph pen had to be reset several times when it ran off the page. At 11:30 p.m., he gamely raised the red and black hurricane flags atop the building. But the flags went unnoticed. The hurricane was already whirling through town.

By then, there was neither time nor place to take refuge. The awesome roar of the wind, crashing of glass and banging of flying objects startled the townspeople. The wind shredded Miami's popular and colorful canvas awnings into countless flapping strips. Some were turned into wind-filled spinnakers that lifted the metal frames from the walls and turned them into battering rams.

For the next six and a half hours, the storm ravaged Miami. Then, at 6:10 a.m., the wind died suddenly. A weary populace breathed a sigh of relief, said a prayer and poured out into the littered streets. Richard Gray ran out into the street screaming, "Seek cover, the storm's not over — it's not over!" Most of the people thought he was 'daft.' But Gray was right. The calm was

Cruisers and other boats were washed far ashore and required a major effort of tow trucks to get them back to sea. Many were damaged beyond repair. *Miami News*.

Fishing on Washington Avenue

Writer Jane Wood Reno, mother of State Attorney Janet Reno, was a young girl living in Miami Beach during the 1926 hurricane. She slept through the first half of the storm; but like so many others, she was caught outside when the lull ended abruptly. It took an hour for her to fight her way home — a total of six blocks. As she pushed against the wind and wall of rain, she stopped just long enough to pick up an exhausted two-foot-long snapper swimming up Washington Avenue. She carried him the rest of the way home, and he became the family dinner.

only the eye of the hurricane, and at 6:45, the "second storm" hit — even worse than the "first storm." The wind picked up as suddenly as it stopped — this time from the opposite direction. Many were trapped out in the storm and lost their lives.

Within an hour, the anemometer atop Miami Beach's Alison Hospital clocked 128 miles per hour winds and blew away. (Gray estimated gusts to 150 miles per hour.) Then came the storm tides. The ocean — eight to nine feet high — washed completely across Miami Beach and pushed itself all the way to Miami. Boats were deposited two blocks from the bay. On the Miami River, an 11-foot wall of water (a bore) pushed upstream, lifting boats that had sought safe harbor and dashing them to bits.

By noon, the storm had moved to Hollywood, Fort Lauderdale and Moore Haven on Lake Okeechobee, but it was all over in Miami. (Before it blew itself out near Biloxi, Mississippi, Pensacola would also feel its fury.)

The toll was enormous, and those 12 hours changed the course of Miami's entire history. The Florida East Coast railroad offered free passage to those who wanted to leave, and many took the railroad up on its offer. Others lost everything they owned, including family and friends.

The nation and the world responded. The Cuban people were particularly generous. Immediately after the storm, the Cuban government sent a battleship to Miami loaded to the gunwales with 250 tons of provisions and supplies along with 50,000 complete doses of typhoid vaccine. Dr. F.M. Fernandez, Secretary of the Havana Public Health Department, and General Miguel Varona, President of the Cuban Red Cross, arrived on the ship, bringing $6,000 raised by the Cuban people. They joined doctors from Miami and others who came in on a relief train from the north. After President Calvin Coolidge asked the nation to send help to Florida, the Red Cross raised more than $3 million.

If you talk to someone who survived the 1926 hurricane, they will talk about the terror and the destruction — but they will also talk about the spirit. As people emerged to pick up the pieces of their lives, signs appeared —

"Down But Not Out"

"Wiped Out but Still Smiling"

"No Increase in Prices, If You're Destitute, It's Free."

People looked out for each other and never hesitated when a stranger needed help.

The cleanup effort was massive. Every able-bodied man was expected to work. Black men were conscripted into work forces

Workers pose in front of the remains of a "pressing shop" on September 18, 1926. Buildings could be replaced, but the trees were often marked by the brunt of the storm for years. *Miami News*.

Measuring the Wrath

Today the U.S. Weather Bureau measures hurricanes on the Saffir-Simpson hurricane scale. One is the mildest, five is the most severe. The 1926 hurricane was a four. There have only been two in the area that have rated a five — the 1935 Keys hurricane and 1969's Camille, which hit Mississippi and Alabama.

whether they wanted to be or not. Miami's people needed a large dose of hope, but in some cases, their extreme optimism backfired and slowed down the relief effort or caused Miamians to be criticized for caring more about the tourist season than its own people.

Miami's devastation was recorded in a pictorial book, *The Florida Hurricane and Disaster*, by L.F. Reardon only three months after the tragedy. It told the story with all its drama, pathos and blood-curdling reality. Although it recorded only nine days, it painted a picture that could not be forgotten. Reardon's account of the storm and its aftermath still stands alone. The pictures and his own experiences told it all, complete with the immediate and constant front-page editorials that appeared daily in every local paper.

Aftermath

On October 20, just when Miami was beginning to lose its bombed-out appearance, word came that another hurricane was on its way. The wrath of God seemed unending. This time, the people responded even though forecaster Richard Gray said it was "impossible" for the hurricane to hit Miami. Crowds stormed the Florida East Coast Railroad ticket windows, trying to get out of town. Those who stayed boarded up every window in sight, and over 20,000 people sought refuge in hurricane shelters. The storm just missed hitting Miami directly, but 650 people were killed as it crossed Cuba.

In the 60 years since the 1926 hurricane, more than 13 storms have visited South Florida. Some hit directly, causing great damage; others simply grazed the coast.

The 1928 storm was as hard on Palm Beach as the 1926 was on Miami and almost wiped out Belle Glade.

The 1935 Labor Day Keys hurricane is considered by some to be the most severe to hit Florida in modern times. It killed hundreds of veterans who had been hired to build the overseas highway to Key West and mortally wounded Flagler's overseas railroad.

In the middle of the 1945 hurricane, the world's largest wooden blimp hanger at Richmond Field burned to the ground. (Its concrete pilings are still visible at the Metro Zoo.)

The very wet 1947 hurricanes (both of them) flooded Hialeah and the area around the Miami River. (Governor Bob Graham left his Pensuco home via boat from the second floor! This flood prompted the last major Army Corps of Engineers' Everglades drainage project.)

The 1935 hurricane was the only "category 5" hurricane to hit South Florida. It killed hundreds of veterans who were in the Keys to build the overseas highway. Most were buried in a common grave in Miami. *Miami News*.

After the October 1947 hurricane, *Miami Daily News* carriers delivered the evening paper to a Hialeah resident via rubber raft. *Miami News*.

It has been 21 years since Hurricane Betsy came through — 1965 — and she was not a severe storm.

Today we know one thing for sure. A major South Florida hurricane is long overdue. To make matters worse, we are lulled into a false sense of security by advanced hurricane tracking and memories of Hurricane David that, for South Florida, was not a hurricane at all.

But with all the miracles of modern technology, it is still impossible to be 100-percent sure of a storm's path. (In 1964 as the forecasters were reporting that the eye of hurricane Cleo would miss Miami, the wind died abruptly at the weather bureau, and the eye passed over the town.)

It is estimated that if a hurricane of the 1926 variety hit Miami directly today, billions of dollars of damage could be expected with great loss of life. Even though the South Florida building code is one of the strictest in the world, Miami and Miami Beach have changed dramatically since 1965 — waterfront condominiums, houses built on former lowlands or "below the ridge" (as old-timers describe it), Florida Keys developments and glass boxes that have never been tested by a real storm.

National Hurricane Chief Neil Frank commented recently that "we're more vulnerable to a hurricane in South Florida than we have ever been in our history." Perhaps the biggest problem now, as it was then, is complacency. All the scientific advances in the world will not help if people do not listen.

It is hoped that this reprint of L.F. Reardon's *Florida Hurricane and Disaster 1926* will make believers out of all of us. Perhaps it will do for today's reader what Ralph Munroe wished the July 1926 hurricane would do for the people of his day — "put the fear of the Lord into the scoffers."

Arva Moore Parks
September 1986

Miami's 1964 Hurricane Cleo was a minor (category 2) hurricane. It hit Miami dead center and caused damage to storefronts that had not been boarded up — a lesson to us all. *Miami News.*

Miami's last hurricane — Hurricane Betsy — damaged the Orange Bowl stadium and blew down the marquee in 1965. Ironically, the University of Miami Hurricane sign was undamaged. *Miami News.*

The Florida Hurricane and Disaster

L. F. REARDON

Foreword

THIS story of America's most destructive storm is written with the desire to preserve as accurately as possible a record of the facts and conditions faced by those who suffered through the great disaster; an appreciation of the magnanimous response of the American people to our South Florida's sufferers in their hour of need; a detailed account of the relief work done by the various organizations; and a review of the trials and obstacles in the way of reconstruction.

Eleven hours of terror and destruction brought to 300,000 people in South Florida, over an area sixty miles wide and six hundred miles in length, a task without parallel in American history. No greater acts of heroism, suffering or sacrifice have been recorded than the stories of some of those who experienced the wrath of the Hurricane of September 17-18, 1926. This story, written in the form of a diary, together with its accompanying illustrations, is as accurate a testimony of the facts and problems faced as could be had when it was written during the early days of the disaster. No attempt is made to exaggerate or minimize the catastrophe. Written during the days of despondency verging on despair, the effort is still made to show the glimmer of hope and determination in the hearts of South Florida's people once more to restore America's Playground to an even more brilliant spot in the sun.

THE AUTHOR.

This Picture Was Made From the Daily News Building at 7:45 a.m., September 18th, 1926.

SATURDAY, SEPTEMBER 18:

I HAVE just come through Hell. Before placing the day and date at the head of this chronicle, I had to stop and think, cudgel my brain, ponder. I'm not normal. I'm not sure that I'm perfectly sane. My body feels as it would after ten rounds of fighting or three football games. Each foot weighs a ton, and my head is splitting. But we're all here at the Everglades Hotel — Deanie, Mark, Sheila and myself—and the storm has gone over to Alabama.

The Florida Hurricane
America's Greatest Storm

CHAPTER I.

I must set this down now for I'm not sure how long my reason will last. My God, but I'm tired. I'll write it now while every minute's horror of those unforgettable ten hours stands out in my brain like a year in an inferno.

I'll start with yesterday afternoon. That was Friday. I left my office at the Coral Gables Construction Building about four o'clock, to play a round of golf with Johnny Wade, of Boston, on the Country Club course. On the way we bought a copy of the *Miami Tribune* with an eight-column "streamer" heading giving warning of a tropical storm. Of course, we paid little attention. They appear often down here this season of the year. Johnny beat me and we went to my home on Murcia Avenue, west of the Miami-Biltmore golf course. Charlie Becher,

One of the Few Totally Wrecked Buildings in Coral Gables, Which Weathered the Storm Better Than Most Sections in the Hurricane's Path.

Scenes Which Greeted One in Royal Palm Park, Miami, Florida, Saturday Afternoon, September 18th, 1926.

of Winnipeg, and Jack Reeves, of Philadelphia, were there. We had dinner and they stayed until 11 o'clock discussing the future of motion pictures in Miami.

The wind was rising. We locked all windows and barred the double doors leading from the sun parlor to the living room. We were not afraid at this time but considered that the house stands alone on high ground, unsheltered by close or adjoining buildings. The wind was now from the northeast and was steadily gaining in velocity. My first apprehension came when the rising gale tore the awning from the east window of my room, at the northern rear of the house, and whipped the iron weight bar through the glass. Starting up from a doze I went to Mark's bed on the sun porch. He was sleeping, but the wind was slashing at the heavy interior curtains around him. I woke him (he's only eight) and sent him into Deanie's room at the south end. I did the same with Sheila, who is six.

Deanie was reading. Leaving the children there, I returned to my own room to find rain pouring through the broken window. Against the lights on Ferdinand Drive, I could see the tall pines bending before the storm, and across the golf course I dimly made out the outline of the Miami-Biltmore.

For more than an hour the wind blew steadily, and there was not yet any reason for worry. I read, but not for long. A terrific onrush tore the awnings from the entire east side of the house, and the windows of Sheila's room came in with a crash.

Then the lights went out on the street and in all houses. We were left in the blackest dark I have ever seen (there, am I not a little daft?)

to do battle for our lives against the most terrific hurricane known to this peninsula, or the Western Hemisphere.

We groped for the children's clothes and managed to half dress them. Matches were useless as the wind was rushing through the broken windows in the rear rooms and down the hall. The gale had now reached a steady roar, but compared to what was to come, it was a gentle zephyr soughing through the palms. The walls trembled and there was a crash of glass downstairs. What to do — we could not see each other and had to shout to make ourselves heard. Would we stay in the house and take our chances, or go out into the storm? I went down and out the front door on the south end of the house and stepped into the gale. It hurled me several yards and I managed to regain the door by grabbing the awning bars that still were fastened to the side of the house. I knew I could never carry the children fifty yards through that gale, and Deanie is not a strong woman. (I wonder how Gus Mitchell is faring on his houseboat out in the bay.) Groping my way upstairs I found the family had barricaded themselves in Deanie's room against the terrific pressure of the wind coming down the corridor. (That frightful gale must be making 90 miles an hour.) Dark — pitchy, inky darkness. What to do. Every few minutes the roar of the raging storm would rise in a quick crescendo and the walls would tremble.

I pushed the family ahead of me down the corridor to the stairway. Taking one under each arm I went down, and we held a shouting consultation at the back door leading through the laundry to the garage. We would sit in the car so that if the house came down it would fall to-

Scenes Like This Confronted People in the Storm Area Saturday Afternoon, September 18th, 1926—Their Homes in Ruins.

A View of Miami's Bayfront, Sunday Morning, September 19th, 1926.

K. K. K. Building, Southwest Sixth Street and 8th Avenue, With Whitehouse Grocery Ruins on the Ground Floor.

building can stand it.) I got in and extended myself over Deanie and the children to await the crash that surely would come if this wind, which now had risen to 100 miles an hour, would not abate. They always said I had a weak mind and a strong back. Now to prove it. Across the street the Whalens from Boston were signalling through the raging tempest by turning their headlights on and off. They too had taken to the garage. Did they need help? How could I go? I returned the signal. What's that?

Above the roar of the storm, there started a high wail like the sound of an ambulance siren. It could not be that; for we were on the outskirts of Coral Gables, six miles from Miami. The sound rose slowly. I jumped out of the car and went to the door of the garage.

Through the fury of the tempest I could not see the trees twenty feet from the house. Still sang the weird sound. The water! A tidal wave! In my mind I pictured a wall of water sweeping over the city. This is the end. I returned to the car and told Deanie to be *prepared for the worst*—I thought that sound was water. In a few minutes it died down, leaving the dull monotonous deadly roar of the gale. Then it came again—about ten minutes later. Never have I heard a sound that froze one's young blood like that. There was a ripping, tearing crash. A tree—great large pine—fell across the driveway of the garage ten feet from where we sat. Our egress was cut off.

We stayed in the car from two o'clock Saturday morning until seven o'clock. Five hours of torture expecting every moment to be buried under tons of stucco and Cuban tile or swept away entirely. Daylight. Dawn began to break

wards the south and away from us. I had forgotten that the garage, which is attached to the house at its northwest corner, lies below and under some eighteen feet of the two-story structure. But it was the best bet, so we struck out. No sooner had I released the latch of the kitchen door than it shot back and was shattered against the electric range. On our hands and knees we

crawled, holding the children, out through the laundry and down three steps into the shelter of the garage.

I placed the family in the seat of the heavy roadster and threw over the top an old mattress to ward off the blow I was sure would come—for the roof of the garage was made of thin boards. (Wonder if the Meyer-Kiser Bank

West Flagler Street at 12th Avenue, Saturday Morning, September 18th, 1926.

at 5:45 and came at about six o'clock. Never before was it as welcome to us. The raging elements paused. But they were only sparring for breath. The wind died down to almost absolute quiet and we went back into the house. Thank God it was over and we were alive. But our relief was to be of short life.

Believing there would be a run on food, I managed to remove enough wreckage and debris to get the car out of the garage and drove down to Ponce de Leon Boulevard. The scene of wreckage brought tears to my eyes. Coral Gables'

buildings, with a few exceptions, had weathered the terrific blast, but the beautiful foliage was laid low. Light and telephone wires were strewn about in reckless abandon. The ground was covered with green grapefruit. A few weather-beaten policemen were standing about the ruins of destroyed buildings.

I found one grocery store open and spent ten minutes buying staple commodities. I tried to get a bottle of distilled water, for the city water was off. Failed. By the time I had the groceries placed in the rear of the car, the wind had again

risen to about 40 miles per hour. The storm was returning! Filled with fear and dread, I raced the twenty blocks back to my home. The new storm and gale was now coming out of the south-east. I barred all doors and windows on the south end of the house which had escaped the havoc of the night. Inside of five minutes (it was now about eight o'clock Saturday morning) the velocity of the wind had reached eighty miles an hour, and was increasing by the minute. Again, what to do. Would the house withstand this southern gale as well as the one from the north?

Wreckage along Miami River Looking East From 5th Street Bridge. Six Bodies Were Recovered Here, September 18th and 19th, 1926.

The garage was out of the question now for the tempest was tearing through its doors. Upwards, still upwards rose the frightful roar, and steadily it gained velocity. I gathered Deanie and the children close to the front door which was already bending under pressure of the rushing gale. If the house came in now I thought the force of the storm would carry it over our heads to the north. Perhaps we could escape and crawl to the car which was backed to the wind on the driveway thirty feet away. Never abating for an instant the wind rose still higher until it sounded like hundreds of steamer whistles blowing at once. Then came once more the terrifying siren-like moan that had made hideous the previous night. That surely is water, for Biscayne Bay lies only three miles to the southeast! Deanie and I took the children in our arms and waited for the end. With an ear-splitting rush of raging wind the large double doors of the living room flew open and the ripping, tearing hurricane found us. The wind must have been making by this time 120 miles an hour—through the living room of our home. I placed the chil- dren behind a heavy trunk in the hall and crawled along the fireplace to the living room doors.

By strength I never knew I had I managed to force one of the doors closed and placed my foot against it. Reaching for the other, I could only bring it against the terrific wind to within two feet of its mate. Then the plaster fell. A titanic gust of slashing wind picked me up bodily and hurled me against the dining room buffet forty feet distant. This house will not stand another minute! I crawled back to the hall, gathered the

Biscayne Boulevard Looking North From Royal Palm Park, McAllister Hotel, Used as Base Hospital, in Foreground.

children in my arms and motioned Deanie to follow me. We got through the kitchen and out into the laundry. Perhaps that was the best thing to do. Placing the children in the large slate wash-tubs, we covered them with pillows and stood over them, hoping that they would in some way escape. Through the yawning window frames east and west, we could see the tall Australian pines twisting, writhing and tumbling before the rushing wall of wind. The air was streaked with garbage cans, automobile tops, dog-houses, furniture, and parts of buildings. We could barely see the ground because of the rain which was being driven in white singing sheets. The force of the wind inside the house shattered the glass of the kitchen door like the report of a gun above the roar and peppered our backs. Will this cursed storm never abate or is it determined to decimate us and our beautiful city? Hours went by—years of terror. It is now 11 o'clock. The storm maintains its steady roar for five or more minutes only to increase at intervals, and every increase is plainly felt by pains in my ears from the pressure. I hear today it reached 130 miles per hour on the recording instrument of the Allison hospital and blew the instrument away.

I was tired. My legs and back ached after my battle with the double doors. I became indifferent to death and hung on only for the sake of Deanie and the babies. But nothing would happen. The house would not come down. Nothing but the deafening wail of the storm—for four hours until twelve-thirty o'clock.

The morning tempest subsided more slowly than that of the night and we returned for the

Five-Thousand-Ton Freighter and Three Private Yachts Driven by the Storm Into Royal Palm Park, Saturday, September 18th, 1926.

second time into what was a home but now a scene of sickening desolation. Nothing was left. Those three words tell the story.

We packed up our clothes (some were dry in the closets) and started for the Everglades Hotel in Miami. Scenes of the storm's ravages were everywhere. Trees, poles and wires lay across the streets. Cuban tile dotted the scene with dull red splotches. Roofs, whole and intact, were lying blocks from their proper locations. The "Wild-cat," a large general market at Red Road and the Tamiami Trail (Southwest Eighth Street), was flat. Few people were to be seen. Are they all dead? Those we did see were either laughing hysterically or weeping. One grocer stood calmly back of his cash register, his entire store naked to the lowering Florida skies. There were no customers. As we approached Miami

along Eighth Street sights of desolation that met our eyes were heart-rending. Whole sides of apartment blocks had been torn away, disclosing semi-naked men and women moving dazedly about the ruins of their homes. Houses, stores and shops lay sprawled. How many dead are under them? Everybody was looking for a drink of water—and there was none to be had. People were pouring into the street—most of them in bathing suits. Ambulances rushed in every direction, their wailing sirens reminiscent of the storm. There's a boy covered with blood running blindly across the street. Where are his parents? We must turn here as a building has spread itself across the trail. Is that wind rising again?

I am too tired to write any more now. We got to the Everglades Hotel after circling the business district where, for several blocks, the water

was four feet deep and laden with wreckage. The lobby is full of refugees from the storm. Third street is strewn with twisted automobiles. Along Biscayne Boulevard large yachts and barges weighing hundreds of tons have been deposited in front of the McAllister and Columbus Hotels.

We are in a soggy apartment now—and we have had a drink of water. We must sleep; or have I been dreaming a terrible dream?

The declaration of martial law on Saturday afternoon, the day of the hurricane:

PROCLAMATION

To the People of Miami and Vicinity:

Due to the relief work now in progress during the present crisis, it is requested that all those who have no specific business on hand refrain from congesting the main arteries of traffic, in order to facilitate such relief work.

This is not a gala occasion, or a legal holiday, and should not be treated as such. The public can greatly assist relief work by staying off the streets.

The city is under martial law, and those who fail to comply with this proclamation will be subject to arrest and imprisonment.

F. H. WHARTON,
City Manager, City of Miami

Approved:
JAMES H. GILMAN, *Acting Mayor.*
September 19, 1926.

The following orders were issued last night by Maj. Robert N. Ward, to be effective during the period of martial law in Dade county:

1. Martial law is hereby declared this eighteenth day of September, 1926, for the county of Dade, state of Florida.

2. All persons entering Dade county on any highway must obtain a pass from military headquarters or prove they are legal residents of Dade county.

3. No person will be allowed in the streets or in the public highways of Dade county after dark.

4. No gasoline will be sold in the city of Miami without an order from military headquarters.

5. Any person found guilty of profiteering will be prosecuted to the fullest extent of the law.

6. Sightseeing at any hour is absolutely prohibited.

7. No person is to enter Miami over bridges or causeways without a permit from military headquarters.

8. All motor cars will be required to observe state laws regarding ambulances and motor vehicles engaged in service of law enforcement and relief work.

East Flagler Street as It Appeared Sunday Morning, September 19th, 1926.

Ready to Start Over, From Ground Up, After the Storm of September 17th and 18th, in Miami, Florida.

How quickly the people of Miami started rebuilding is reflected in the newspapers published immediately after the hurricane. The Miami Tribune's first streamer line read, "Miami Rebuilding," and its first editorial in their issue of Sunday, September 19th, written by Tom Arnold, is reproduced here:

"Out of the night that covers me,
Black as the pit from pole to pole,
I thank whatever Gods there be
For my unconquerable soul."

THE rewards of adversity are indefinite. Miami has suffered the sting of adversity and out of it her soul has sprung to life. Her citizens are united in one thought: they are of one mind to rebuild their city.

Chicago had her fire, and a new Chicago was born. San Francisco had her earthquake and prospered thereafter. Galveston's premier position in the shipping world today is traceable to a mighty tidal wave which almost annihilated that island city. Adversity struck those cities with such intensity that it seemed their difficulties were insurmountable.

Yet today they are there, visual evidence of the power of men to rebuild what God alone can

Miami's Unconquerable Soul

(AN EDITORIAL)

destroy. Man has never learned why the Almighty sees fit to destroy cities, but man has learned through experience that what is destroyed by fire, earthquake or hurricane, can be rebuilt better than it was originally.

Here is the testing time for Miami and here is her opportunity. The hurricane which swept her and her surrounding sister cities left death, sorrow and desolation in its wake. Only the death cannot be undone. For those whose lives were sacrificed to the elements we mourn.

To those whose lives were spared we commend a constructive course. They must rebuild Miami at any cost in time, money and labor. They will do it, for that work already has started. Too much money is invested here to permit of a desertion of an entire city. Such a course is unthinkable.

Since this is true and since Miami WILL BE REBUILT, shed a tear for the dead you loved, pause a moment over the industrial, commercial or artistic monument you had erected as the pride of your life, and then look bravely to the future. That is the spirit of Miami, out of which a new city will arise to face whatever storms the future shall bring.

From a materialistic standpoint, the storm has done no permanent damage. Its destructive path will be followed by workmen in the thousands, men whose axes and hammers and saws and riveters will resound day and night. This activity will mean prosperity, a prosperity that will outweigh by millions of dollars the millions of dollars in destruction the hurricane has wrought.

The spectacle of an industrious community, doing its own work well where adversity might have discouraged weaker men and women will attract the attention of the entire world. It will bring to Miami specialists and technical men from every walk of life to lend a helping hand. Such help as Miami needs she will receive, gracefully, humbly, thankfully. But she will not fall into the error of depending upon such help, she is not a mendicant, but a full grown city, thankful for the opportunity to rebuild from her wrecked stone and mortar greater structures than those which originally graced the sites upon which the newer ones will be raised.

Upper Left: Used to Be a Seaplane.

Lower Left: Houseboats Determined to Utilize Flagler Street Instead of the Miami River.

Upper Right: Coast Guard Cutter on Biscayne Boulevard, Miami.

Lower Right: Tank Cars and Boats on Bayshore Drive Near the City Docks.

Center: Royal Palm Park with Bandstand at the Left.

SUNDAY, SEPTEMBER 19:

THEY'RE bringing in the dead from Hialeah. All night the ambulances have been screaming along Biscayne Boulevard and through the main streets. The injured are being taken to the McAllister Hotel which is being used as a base hospital. Martial law declared last night. You must have a pass to be in the streets after six o'clock in the evening. Reports have it Miami Beach has been washed completely away and the dead are decomposing in piles of thousands. Both causeways are wrecked and none can cross the Bay, we can only guess yet.

I awoke at nine o'clock. Tom Fortune and Preston Myers were in the apartment with the report that a thousand are dead at Hollywood. No power. No water. We are on the ninth floor. Pity those on the sixteenth. My muscles are stiffening, but I must go and see whether our friends are safe. The babies are clamoring for breakfast, but the apartment is devoid of food. Plenty in the city, I am told.

Charlie Becher and I went over to the Columbus Hotel and met "Tub" Palmer and Roger Nordello. Their first question was did I know anything about Gus Mitchell. They had just returned from one of the Venetian Islands where his yacht the "Elvira" on which he lived had been moored for several months. The yacht was gone and Gus is missing. The island had been swept by the waters of the Bay and many houses were in ruins. Roger and "Tub" were among the few to get through the wreckage on the Venetian causeway. Then it was closed to traffic. Miami Beach is cut off from traffic or communication. We knew Gus would remain

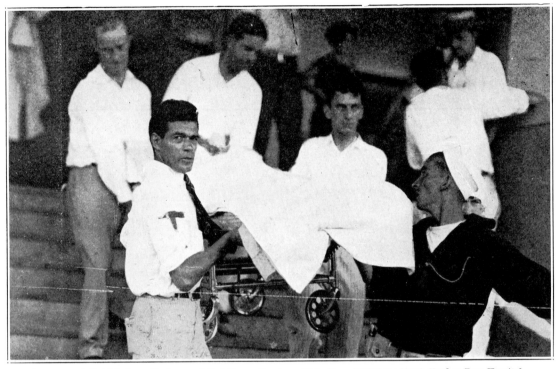

Volunteer Relief Workers, Marines and Red Cross, Bearing a Body From McAllister Hotel, Used as Base Hospital.

The Florida Hurricane
America's Greatest Storm

CHAPTER TWO

on his boat. He has been through many storms in Florida waters. "Spider" Holmes was with him. We had no doubt both were drowned. We can imagine the anxiety of Mrs. Mitchell in Nashville when reports of the hurricane reached her.

Marines from Key West are patrolling the streets; also national guardsmen from up the state. Down at the police station Forrest Nelson, assistant chief, is having scores of special police officers sworn in. There is confusion everywhere. City Manager Wharton is making a speech from the steps of the courthouse, saying the streets are free to everyone regardless of what Major Ward has said. There is a row between the city and the military. Bread lines are forming in front of the downtown Catholic church and the American Legion building on Biscayne Boulevard. It is reported Fort Lauderdale is flat with thousands dead. Newspaper and telegraph offices are jammed with men and

Florida's National Guard Protecting Miami Banks from Looters.

women trying to connect with the outside world or find trace of missing relatives. But there are no wires and no "juice." Miami is alone with its tragedy. No, not alone. Al Reck, a *Miami Tribune* reporter, slashed his way through the debris on the Dixie Highway to West Palm Beach Saturday and gave the world its first news of the hurricane.

Still come the dead. King's undertaking parlors are full of corpses. There are twenty bodies at Philbrick's and eleven at Comb's. Hundreds of cars have been pressed into service as ambulances. The Red Cross is organizing.

Flagler Street is a mass of debris, but the buildings are standing. All the plate glass in Burdine's store has been crashed in and goods on all floors water soaked. All signs are strewn about the streets. The great sign atop the First National Bank is hanging over at a dangerous angle and the street between First and Second Avenues is roped off. Parts of roofs, poles and wires are about the pavement and everywhere broken glass. The city and county *jails stood up* under the gale and were the *safest spots* in Dade

County. Not a building in the downtown district is undamaged. Northeast First Street was as badly hit as Flagler. The Meyer-Kiser Bank Building is leaning perilously and the street is closed. Jack Reeves tells me he watched the antics of this seventeen-story building from the door of the Ritz hotel. He says it waved its tail like a porpoise and did a sort of charleston during the gale. They say it must be taken down. Cromer-Cassell's new department store at Miami Avenue and First Street has a ruined ground floor and a stock of wet goods. Somebody said the Exchange Building was leaning, but I can't see it. First and Second Avenues look as if some titanic destroyer had passed along swinging a gigantic club of destruction. Gangs of boys are betting on whether the next building they come to will have any plate glass left.

Just like playing "Beaver." The interior of offices are nakedly apparent from the streets, the walls and roofs having been ripped off and spread over many blocks. Fred Rand's Roosevelt Hotel is a mess.

Seventeen people died huddled together in one building at Hialeah. Reports that Homestead has been wiped from the earth. Two hundred are dead at Moore Haven on the south shores of Lake Okeechobee. The Bay gave up six more bodies in the last three hours. The Miami river defies description. Hundreds of yachts and houseboats are in ruins. Bodies will be rising for the next three days. "Doc" Moreau's "Silent Night," formerly owned by Secretary Mellon, was reduced to floating spars. Biscayne Boulevard and Royal Palm Park resemble an annual yacht show. A five-masted schooner weighing several thousand tons is beached at the foot of

Sixth Street with its bow close to the entrance of the *Miami Daily News* Building. It will be days before the county causeway is passable. We tried to cross to Miami Beach by way of the Venetian Causeway, but everyone was turned back. It will be open this afternoon at three o'clock, to those who have official passes. Thousands of hysterical men and women are crowding the approaches to the causeways. Not a word yet from Miami Beach.

Property damage is estimated from $50,000,000 to $500,000,000. Nobody knows and nobody *cares much* until the dead are buried and the injured cared for. Automobiles are rushing through the streets bearing crudely painted warnings, "Boil Your Drinking Water." But there is no drinking water except what can be bought in bottles, and that is hard to get. We went to five soda fountains and met the same information—"Sold Out." Physicians already have used most of the typhus and tetanus antitoxin and immunization. More is coming by airplane. Not a telephone is working in the Miami district. Linemen are going to work. Those are the boys needed now. There go a gang of prisoners released from jail to hack the way for relief food and medical cars to get to Hollywood, Dania and Fort Lauderdale.

Poor Hialeah! I have just returned from what is considered Miami's stormiest suburb even when there is no hurricane. Greater havoc could not be wrought by a corps of Big Berthas. Through Miami's northwest section hundreds of workingmen's homes have been razed to the ground. Furniture and bedding were scattered for miles by the terrific force of the gale. Piles of wreckage and naked floors mark the locations

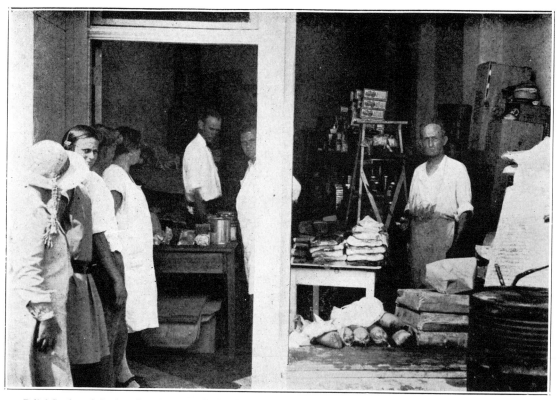

Relief Station of the American Legion in Legion Building, Bayshore Drive, Opened Sunday Morning, September 19, 1926.

of what were cozy little homes. Bedraggled women are trying to gather together the remnants of their household goods.

Little children are running about naked. Thank God for the Florida climate! Haggard men are searching the wreckage for—what? But they smile, those people. Above three wrecked homes the Stars and Stripes are waving gently in the breeze.

Our way along the river is blocked by poles, yachts and wreckage from the stream. We have to cut through the golf course of the Miami

Country Club to Allapattah Drive. Desolation is all about. Few houses or business blocks weathered the frightful persistence of the storm. Telephone and light poles are down the entire length of 36th Street, from Allapattah Drive to Hialeah. So we proceed slowly to 44th Street and west. The White Belt Dairy is in ruins. Many met death in this section. Hialeah is bravely pulling itself together, counting its dead and rushing its injured to five standing buildings where doctors and nurses are dead on their feet after 24 hours without sleep or rest. The

A View of Northeast First Street Elevation of the Meyer-Kiser Bank Building, Showing Part of the Damage Sustained.

water is four feet deep in some places. The Administration Building and offices of James Bright and Glen Curtis stood out against the elements but every window was broken and many of the beautiful Spanish embellishments torn away. The club house of the Hialeah Country Club is missing. Arthur Pryor's home still stands undamaged on 36th Street. Willie Willie's Seminole Indian Village was swept clean but there were no deaths or injuries here for the houses were of thatch made of palm leaves. Chief Willie Willie's mother, 84 years old, and born at Hialeah, said it was the worst storm in her memory. On to the race track and what a sight! Damage to America's finest racing plant cannot be estimated until Joe Smoot returns from the North. The roof of the great grandstand was ripped off and strewn over the Everglades. Many of the stables are demolished and the fences are gone. One side of the club house caved in. The dog-track suffered less damage, but the Jai-Alai Fronton was scooped out through its roof, which has departed this section of the country. Jimmie Hodges' building where the Miami Follies girls frollicked in the glare of the spotlights resembles what was left of the Rheims cathedral after the German bombardment. No sacrilege meant.

Details of the storm's destructive force at Hialeah are given in the following eyewitness story of the hurricane written by Al Reck, of the *Miami Tribune,* which managed to publish four pages today on the press of the *Palm Beach Times:*

Eyewitness Writes of Storm

Miami Friday night and Saturday went through Hell.

Today it is looking over the ruins, checking up on the dead, caring for the injured and fighting to avoid

Drying Stock on Roof of Burdine's Department Store, Damaged by Water.

that which usually follows a terrible disaster—pestilence and disease.

At two o'clock Saturday morning the hurricane, cutting a path of death from the Carribean, hit Miami with all its force. It was a 130-mile-an-hour gale—the worst South Florida or the entire United States has ever known.

Early Friday Miami was warned of the approaching hurricane. She had ridden through one this year and rather looked with uplifted eyebrows at warnings of a second blow. Forecaster Gray, of the U. S. Weather Bureau, said that Miami would probably feel a 45-mile-

an-hour gale. He refused to say that there would be a hurricane despite the fact that news dispatches from Washington and Jacksonville said that the blow would probably be one of the worst that South Florida had ever known.

Still there were some who took the warning to heart. All day Friday a steady stream of small boats steamed and chugged their way to safe anchorage up the Miami river. Many of them are still there, others are gone—many others.

At 8 o'clock Friday night the first gusts of wind filled Miami's eyes with dust. It was light. But it continued

First Relief Train to Reach Devastated Miami Over F. E. C. Sunday, September 19th, 1926, Twenty-four Hours After the Hurricane.

Showing Results of the Storm at Palm Avenue and 23rd Street in Hialeah, Florida; Jai-Alai Fronton Partly Unroofed at the Left. Many Deaths and Injuries Occurred Near Here.

—heavier and still heavier. At ten o'clock I made my way down to the center of Miami. It was hard going even then. The wires were not down and messages told of the storm on the way.

I called the Tropical Radio station at Hialeah on the phone and Mr. Bourne, the manager, informed me that Nassau was silent. The queen of the Bahamas had evidently been struck by the gale already. Bimini, he said, had dismantled their station at six o'clock. The wireless station at Nassau had evidently been blown down.

It had started to rain. I dropped over in the sheriff's office and found the county police force wondering just how bad the hurricane was going to be or if it really was going to hit Miami.

Going on back to that apartment house where I live, I found the tenants gathered in frightened and wondering groups.

We talked until midnight, wondering whether we were really going to see a storm or not. All the time the wind grew in intensity. At one o'clock it was howling and roaring like a hungry lion.

At two o'clock, with the weather outside as black as ink and the wind humming like an elevated train, the power and lights went off.

Fifteen minutes later there was a terrible crash. With flashlight we started from the ground floor, made our way to the third floor only to be met with a shower of brick and mortar. The roof had gone from the building.

Minutes later, it seemed like hours, another terrific gust of wind, another crash brought the walls of the third floor crashing onto the second. In the lobby of the building were all the tenants. Braces were placed against the doors but even then the wind was not to be denied. The window glass blew in and the rain came in torrents.

Until six o'clock we huddled in the lobby, wet from the driven and dripping water. Then the storm subsided. Light came in the east.

Looking around with fearful eyes, all I could see were wrecked and ruined homes.

I made my way down to the center of Miami from Twentieth street N. W. to Miami avenue—as far as I traveled—was a mass of debris. Many buildings were still standing but this was before the second blow struck.

Streets downtown were flooded with water driven in from the bay.

All wires were down. Miami was cut off from outside communication. There was only one possible way to get word to the rest of the country of Miami's condition and that was by radio. I thought that the wireless station at Hialeah, operated by the Tropical Radio station, might be able to get a message out.

Automobiles that had been left on the streets were either wrecked or drowned out. It was next to impossible to obtain any sort of transportation. Finally I managed to meet the superintendent of a taxicab company. He agreed to attempt the trip to Hialeah.

We started out. That taxi driver was gifted with the luck of the gods. As we sped out north from Miami, past scenes of ruin and desolation on every hand, it seemed as if the wind-strained trees and telephone poles threw themselves at us but missed. The driver literally hurtled the machine over fallen trees and poles. We smashed wires by the mere strength of the heavy taxi and finally reached the radio station.

There was a heart-rending sight. Refugees, who had lost their all in the hurricane, had gathered at the station for safety—the wireless buildings, three in number, were constructed of steel and concrete. The huge towers were flat on the ground. One of them had smashed its way through the operator's dormitory.

Tiny children were crying in the arms of their parents. None of the refugees were dressed except in night clothes or clothing hastily donned. They were wet, injured and miserable.

One woman had her leg broken above the ankle. We bandaged it the best we could with cloth torn from shirts. Another had a shoulder broken. A man had a broken left leg and two ribs smashed. One boy, about 12 years of age, was so badly cut in the leg by broken glass that we had to put a tournequet around his leg.

The wireless operators joined in and made hot coffee. There was no food.

Three men were braced against the door to hold it

Bringing Injured to Community Church in Hialeah, Used as a Hospital, Saturday Afternoon, September 18th.

shut. Then the storm changed and came from the south. This time it was real.

Peering from the rain-clouded windows I could see houses rolling along the ground like tin cans. A figure crawled on hands and knees towards the wireless station. The hurricane was bounding along the ground, hugging it close and driving the rain in a straight line, parallel with the ground.

Making its way to the windward of the wireless station, the figure knocked on a window. We opened it and there was a man about 60 years old.

Nine people were in a house about a block away. One of them, a woman, had a broken leg. They needed help.

The taxi driver was game.

"Let's go," he said.

There was nothing else to do. I went with him.

How it stood up, I don't know and can't realize, but the sturdy taxicab, weaving and swaying in the wind,

dug its way across fields to the house, a one-story frame structure.

The driver backed the stern end of the taxi to the house. We forced the door open, carried the woman with the broken leg out to the cab, loaded three adults and five children in the taxi and started. As we did, the house, in which the nine had been less than 30 seconds before, turned over and started rolling after the cab.

The taxi driver and one of the men in the party carried the injured woman to the wireless station after we had backed our way there. I picked up a child about three years of age.

I had to kneel down and lean over to buck the gale. The wind-driven rain stung like a thousand bees. It cut like a knife and tore my raincoat to ribbons. A gust of extra heavy wind came swooping and bounding, picked my feet up and hurled me a good twenty feet

Refugees at Community Church in Hialeah, Many of Whom Were Made Orphans by the Storm.

and then started me rolling. I held on to the child with one hand and grasped at a palmetto bush with the other. I regained my feet and crawled on my hands and knees to the station with the child.

Once inside we learned that there were at least 30 others out in the storm and had been crouching in the palmettos for hours.

"Let's go," said the taxi driver, and we went.

Out a window to the windward we slipped. The gale picked up the taxi driver and hurled him high in the air. How many trips we made back and forth to the wireless station I do not know, but we found about 30 men, women and children, blue and cold, in the palmettos, gripping the earth to save from getting hit by flying debris.

About three o'clock the gale subsided.

Medical supplies and food were badly needed, so the taxi driver and I started back to town. We drove through Hialeah. There was a picture of ruin. The race track stables were ripped and torn. The Jai-Alai Fronton was shattered as if by a heavy bombardment. Jimmy Hodges' huge cabaret building was lying in ruins. And all around were buildings overturned or wrecked. Not a whole structure was standing.

Supplies Furnished to Refugees in Woodlawn Tourist Camp. Hundreds of Residents in the Tourist Camps Were Without Shelter After the Storm.

Supplies Furnished by Knights of Columbus Relief to Storm Sufferers in Little River Section.

Rumors of the wildest sort flew from lip to lip through the blackness of the tropical night. Another storm was coming. A tidal wave was predicted. Smallpox and typhoid fever had broken out. Men were being shot down for refusing to work. These and many other sensational rumors were somewhat neutralized by the following admonition from Major Robert N. Ward:

DO NOT BELIEVE RUMORS.

Police, city and military officials are cooperating with Miami newspapers in every way to assist in accurate compilation of all facts concerning the effects of the storm.

Lists of dead and injured are being published as rapidly as they are definitely checked. All news is being published with no attempt to minimize or exaggerate conditions. We are publishing the truth as learned from actual conditions.

Get the truth in the newspapers: Do not believe the rumors heard throughout the city and spread by irresponsible persons.

By Order of
MAJOR ROBERT N. WARD,
Commanding Dade County.

Proclamation!

The following proclamation was issued yesterday afternoon by F. H. Wharton, city manager, and James H. Gilman, acting mayor:

To the People of Miami:

We have just passed through the worst storm in the history of our city. A crisis is at hand. In the past we have met and overcome conditions which at first seemed as bad and possibly worse. Why not now?

Many persons, rich and poor, have been rendered homeless and penniless. Through it all they have maintained a calm feeling which is a manifestation of the same spirit upon which the civic development of our city is built.

Our merchants have come to the front of our relief committees with their storehouse supply of food, clothing, etc. They have made a thorough check and find that enough supplies are available to enable the city and its loyal population to carry on for at least thirty days to sixty days. . . .

The banks are in excellent condition. Clerks and officials are working faithfully through long hours of tedious labor to care for the needs of deserving cases. We have requested all banks, through orders for martial law, to supervise carefully all drafts for money, and to require that all withdrawals be for necessaries only, that the best interests of the masses be conserved.

Communication with the outside world has been established through the vigilance of telegraph companies and private radio owners. All extra relief, aside from what is available locally, will be forthcoming within forty-eight hours.

The people of other cities have had experiences similar to ours; they have put their shoulders to the wheel, overlooked trifles, and have rebuilded even greater than before.

Thousands of visitors will be with us during the coming winter, and we have plenty of time in the three months now coming to make ample preparations for their care and entertainment.

We wish to thank personally each person who has assisted in relief work and in the maintenance of peace, harmony and good feeling in the community. . . . Your loyalty is now being tested.

JAMES H. GILMAN, *Acting Mayor.*
F. H. WHARTON, *City Manager.*

America's Finest Race Track and Stables Fared Badly in the Raging Winds.

Wreckage and Destruction Around the Dog Racing Track in Hialeah.

Rum Runners Have no Fear of This Coast Guard Cutter Beached on Miami's Bayfront.

.The Nohab, Once Owned by Ex-Kaiser Wilhelm and One of the Finest Yachts Afloat, Capsized in Biscayne Bay During the Storm. Only one Member of the Crew was Saved.

After Forty-eight Hours' Separation by the Storm, Husband and Wife Meet in Hialeah.

Monday, September 20:

THE city is waking to the horrors of the disaster. All of yesterday there was a spirit of hysterial joking, except among those actively engaged in relief work. Miami has met with perhaps the greatest catastrophe in the history of this country since the Johnstown flood and we might as well admit to the outside world. One reason for the prevailing levity Sunday among those who had not lost relatives in the titanic blast was the absence of any communication. Telephones and telegraphs are things of the past and future. Details were not to be had; none yet knew the facts. Candles flickered last night in homes and apartments. Bonfires illuminated the ruins of houses as the former occupants slept in the open and awoke this morning to renewed realization of their loss.

Declaration of martial law at Miami Beach Sunday:

CITY MANAGER'S PROCLAMATION.

Martial law is declared in Miami Beach.

Everyone Must Be Off the Streets at 6 O'Clock.

We will deal harshly with anyone who profiteers on food or any commodity.

No food, water or other necessity will be sold without first obtaining a permit at the City Hall.

No motor cars shall move without a permit.

There is a supply of drinking water on hand to last at least four days, at which time it is believed that plenty will be available.

Food supplies are also believed sufficient.

Dr. Roche is in charge of sanitation. All available nurses and doctors should report to him immediately at the Alladin building.

Cliff Sawyer is in charge of the wholesale food distribution.

All men who can should report at the city hall to clear the wreckage and to volunteer for police duty.

C. A. Renshaw, *City Manager.*

Picture Made at South Ocean Drive, Miami Beach, Florida, Between Storms Saturday Morning at 7:00, Sept. 18, 1926.

The Florida Hurricane
America's Greatest Storm

Chapter Three

Estimates of the dead range from 150 to 500 in Miami, Hialeah, Miami Beach, Little River, Coconut Grove and Homestead. At Hollywood many corpses lie in improvised undertaking parlors. Details of Fort Lauderdale's travail are slowly seeping through. They say the beautiful little city is level with hundreds dead.

Out at Moore Haven, in the far reaches of the Everglades, the reports are 150 dead. The raging waters of Lake Okeechobee whipped by the northern gale, swept over the dykes and flooded the quiet little town to a depth of fifteen feet. A relief train is being rushed from Sebring. Two families at Moore Haven lost five children each. Residents took to the roofs of their homes only to be washed into the rushing waters of the lake or to see their friends and neighbors drown. At Moore Haven there is no food, no drinking water, no power, no light, and the waters are not receding.

Crowds Being Turned Back at Venetian Causeway, Who Are Attempting to Pass to Miami Beach, September 19, 1926. Only Those Armed With Passes Were Allowed to Cross.

Commodore Stoltz's Beautiful One-Hundred-Foot Yacht Wrecked and Driven Against Venetian Causeway Bridge at Belle Isle, Miami Beach, September 18th.

Gus Mitchell tottered into the Columbus Hotel yesterday afternoon. His experiences in the gale as it swept over Venetian Islands defy narration. Together with "Spider" Holmes he left his yacht at one o'clock Saturday morning. They thought they could make it, to Lee Rumsey's home on Belle Isle. By this time, the surging water was waist high, and the wind making at least 80 miles an hour. It was pitch dark. The island is about two blocks wide, by eight blocks long. They could not discern its banks, and feared stepping into the bay. The wind rose higher and still higher. They staggered through the militant water, which soon was up to their necks, until they came to a house sheltering two women and one man. In ten minutes the house came in. The five persons managed to tie themselves together with bed sheets and struggled out into the teeth of the awful wind that by now was washing high waves over the island. Thus they fought the elements for more than two hours, not knowing what direction they were proceeding or how soon they would be swallowed in the furious waters of the Bay. Praying for daylight they persevered and at five o'clock reached another house where they remained until the storm from the northeast was past.

I went to Miami Beach this morning. In order to cross the Venetian causeway I had to show a police and newspaper pass and promise to return to Miami before dark. My first view of the storm's ravages at America's Playground brought tears to my eyes. Beautiful Belle Isle is prostrate. The homes of Lee Rumsey, J. C. Penney and "Junior" Matthews withstood the gale but present a sorry sight with their shattered windows and ruined furniture. I am told the great

Lower Left: A View of Ocean Frontage Showing Destruction   Lower Center: The Remains of Cook's Bath House at 5th Street   Lower Right: Remains of a Laundry at South Miami Beach, After
Wrought to Palms and Shrubbery on Miami Beach.   and Ocean Drive, Miami Beach.   the Storm of September 17th and 18th, 1926.

pipe organ in the Penney home was damaged beyond repair. All royal palms are down. The Bay front from the causeway to Carl Fisher's Flamingo Hotel is stark naked. Commodore Stolz's 100-foot yacht is in ruins, and partly sunk against the masonry of the causeway. The canal from Belle Isle to Meridian Avenue is half full of wreckage from the Mayflower Hotel, and the new Boulevard Hotel, of the Fisher interests, which was opened a month ago. The building itself weathered the tempest. The glass dome is

gone from the Flamingo and the furniture in the lobby and ground floors damaged.

Vernon Knowles and myself were looking for Charles Gray, famous strike mayor of Winnipeg, who was living with his family in an apartment block at Meridian Avenue and 15th Street. As we crossed the canal into Meridian Avenue our car plunged into three feet of standing water. All about us were fallen trees, poles, wires and the remains of beautiful homes. We found the Grays, haggard but safe. The roof of

their apartment had been blown away, but their furniture was only slightly damaged. Mr. Gray told me the water of the Atlantic Ocean, five blocks east, was six feet deep in Meridian Avenue at the height of the hurricane.

We proceeded through scenes of desolation to South Beach. Here is where the gale did its worst. It took the Coney Island of Miami Beach, twisted and gnarled it into an unrecognizable mass and flung it down on the sands. Hardee's and Smith's Casinos might as well have

Bathing Casino at South Miami Beach on the Morning After the Hurricane. Nearly Everyone Who Has Ever Been in Miami for the Past Few Years Has Used this Casino.

Roney Plaza Hotel on the Ocean Front at 23rd Street, Miami Beach. Note Large Electric Pole Blown Entirely Out of the Ground on Which Couple Are Sitting.

N. B. T. Roney, Miami Beach Developer, Helps Remove Sand From His "Roney Plaza" Hotel.

been under a barrage of heavy cannon for days. The Million Dollar Pier is damaged. The South Beach Casino is tottering, and has been condemned. Charley's Grill is a shell. The Ritz restaurant is no more. The Seabreeze Grill has been razed and its furnishings have gone out to sea. Ocean Drive, from Smith's Casino to Fifth Street, resembles a Belgian town after a siege of many days. Not an apartment block, hotel or storage on South Beach escaped the ravages of the storm. Sand is two feet deep on Ocean Drive from Fifth Street north to the Snowden estate. They are pulling out the dead from the ruins of the casinos and shops. The number will never be known.

Collins Avenue is a pathetic thoroughfare. I have lived in Miami and Miami Beach three years, but had difficulty in knowing when we had arrived at the corner of Collins Avenue and Lincoln Road. We were used to heavy trees and foliage on Collins Avenue. Now it is swept clean on both sides and houses never before ex-

posed to the street are standing in all of their shorn immodesty. The old Carl Fisher home, recently bought by N. B. T. Roney, formerly of Camden, New Jersey, stands naked and badly damaged, the yard strewn with dead fish. The frame home of Mayor Snedigar is intact, but Edna's furniture is a mess. The St. John's Casino, now owned by "Newt" Roney, was completely undermined by the plunging ocean and will have to come down. The entire three blocks of Ocean Drive between the Casino and the Pancoast Hotel were washed away and the ocean waves today are licking the walls of the Wofford Hotel. Dead and decaying fish everywhere. So clean was the sweep of the torrent through the ground floor of the Roney Plaza Hotel that not a tittle of testimony remains, that only two days ago there were here dozens of smart shops, beauty parlors and drug stores. Indian Creek is filled with debris for many yards north of its southern bank. The luxurious offices of Mr. Roney are a complete wreck. Sand of the beach is a foot deep at the rear of the Roney Plaza two hundred yards west of the ocean. As we go north, we see the east top wall of the Pancoast Hotel crashed in. The home of Thomas J. Pancoast, one of the founders of Miami Beach, on Indian Creek, was miraculously saved. Proceeding farther north we are forced to leave our car on Ocean Drive one block from the ocean. It seems the entire beach line has been moved a block west and the sand makes driving impossible. We pass the home of William F. Whitman, Chicago publisher. The house fought the storm with some success, but the seawall and heavy masonry of the front yard are gone. Next we come to a heap of ruins, the home of E. R.

Thomas. Not a foot of the quaint white frame residence is standing. I was looking for the home of Clayton Sedgwick Cooper, at which I have visited many times. So obliterating was the storm that I walked two blocks beyond where it stood. It took me several minutes to orientate myself before I came upon it. What a pity! Here was what I considered Miami's most attractive home. It was furnished throughout in Oriental style—original and fantastic pieces, brought over many years ago by Mrs. Cooper from the Far East. At the rear and on the second floor was the study and library of Mr. Cooper, author of international repute. The Cooper home was so thoroughly destroyed that you would hardly realize a house had stood there. Oriental tapestry and furnishings were scattered for blocks, most of them damaged beyond reclamation. Not a book was to be seen! The dusky Martha was gathering up what fragments were to be found. She had been rescued from the Cooper home one minute before it collapsed, by the Pattersons, next door. The Patterson home was built of poured concrete, but this means nothing in the turbulent life of an ocean. When the wind was rising they barricaded their downstairs doors and windows. In an half-hour the storm was whipping great waves against the front of the house and the Pattersons went to the second story. The entire front of the house, which was of nine rooms, came in with a deafening crash and the roaring ocean tore its way through and past. Mr. and Mrs. Patterson rushed to a small room at the rear upstairs. None too soon for within a few minutes the front section of the roof fell on the ruins of the first floor. By this time the ocean water was 10 feet high for a block from the

Hotel Pancoast on the Ocean Front at Miami Beach, Showing Damage to the Rear Wing.

beach and great, thundering waves were crashing on the North Beach homes and their terrified occupants. The door of the small room sheltering the Pattersons would bend under the impact of the rolling waters, but it held and they were saved. In the lull of the hurricane center Saturday morning they picked their way downstairs in time to see looters disappearing with their food and groceries.

The Ashby home, next door, was flattened and

Mr. Patterson tells me he thinks the negro maid is buried in the ruins.

The magnificent estate of Harvey S. Firestone, tire magnate, far up on the North Beach, sustained damage that cannot yet be computed. The ocean washed over its entire length and breadth, carrying away garages and outhouses, obliterating masonry, decimating trees and shrubbery, ruining the furniture and, it is reported, drowning two servants.

The home of Mark Reardon, of New York,

Residence of Mr. Collins, Son of One of Miami Beach's Pioneers, Wrecked Beyond Repair. The Montmartre School is Located Across the Canal From This Home.

race horse owner and sportsman, was cut in two as if by a knife.

The central and bay-front sections of Miami Beach fared better because of the shallow waters of Biscayne Bay. The northern storm of the night did not have the great bulk of water to toss up that the southern hurricane of Saturday morning had to play with. Carl Fisher's King Cole Hotel sustained only broken windows and water-soaked furniture. Water of the Bay washed up as high as the lobby of the Nautilus Hotel and paused. The home of Frank P. Fildes, publisher of the *Miami Tribune,* was ruined internally, while the home of Robert Weede, a half block north, was unharmed.

Two hundred injured are being cared for at the Allison Hospital and the Floridian Hotel. Sanitary conditions which were a threatening menace after the hurricane, have been improved by pumping salt water through the mains. Drinking water is being issued, two gallons to a family, from the city reservoir and from trucks brought from Miami and West Palm Beach. The dead on Miami Beach are estimated as high as one hundred this afternoon. The Bay will be giving up bodies for days. Many are buried in the sunken ruins of yachts and houseboats. Martial law was declared yesterday but partly removed today.

Maury and Gladys Orr are safe with Little Billy after an experience that will rattle in Maury's memory until the grave. When the ocean rushed them from their feet in their home at Collins Avenue and 34th Street they took to the road. Then the house collapsed. A gigantic wave flung them into a coconut tree where they hung for four hours until the raging elements were tired. Mrs. Orr is a nervous wreck. Old Nellie, nurse to Billy, lies at the point of death in Allison Hospital. Heard tonight that Mary Bullen is returning from Paris to view the ruins of her home near the Miami Beach Country Club. Thank heaven there are no poor people on Miami Beach.

Four trucks laden with food have just come over the Venetian Causeway and drawn up before the Police Station.

This letter, written by a Miami Beach resident, is reproduced by consent:

"My dear Mother:

"I sent you a telegram, or rather filed one to be sent, stating that we are safe; now I will tell you of my last two days' experiences in the storm.

"On Friday evening, about 10:30, I drove down to the foot of 5th street, Miami Beach, to Cook's Casino, with the boys, so that they could see the ocean waves before going to bed, and we walked around to the ocean side of the building where we watched the waves come in and break. We were somewhat disappointed because they were not equal to the ones in the July storm, so we only stayed a few minutes and I took them home.

"We went to bed about 11:15 after pulling up all of the awnings and shutting the windows down as the

This Well Located Near Spanish Village Was Popular Place for First Three or Four Days After the Hurricane. Drinking Water Was Scarce.

Crowds Trying to Get Food and Water Permits Monday, September 20th, 1926. Chief Henning Handled Situation in a Most Commendable Manner.

wind was then blowing quite hard but not alarmingly so, and all of us went to sleep.

"At 1:30 Mr. Hukle, who lives downstairs in the apartment, knocked sharply on the door and stated that he was getting uneasy as the storm was getting worse steadily and thought everyone should get up and dress. Mr. Nelson of Minneapolis was already up and as he passed our door also called in and agreed with Mr. Hukle.

"The children were still asleep. Howard and Walker dressed, as did Ruth and myself, but Wayne, who is only six, refused to be disturbed, so I wrapped him in a blanket and we joined the other occupants of the apartment, all of whom had already gathered in the downstairs hall, some with their clothes over pajamas, some only partly clothed. And with reinforced concrete walls and floor above us and heavy fire doors behind us closed, we sat on the cement stairsteps and waited.

"By 2 o'clock the wind, which had steadily increased, had reached a velocity of over a hundred miles per hour, and some of the awnings were being torn off the building—tile from the roof were being torn off and pieces crashed down on the steps of the entrance of the building. A window gave way with a crash, and the onrush of wind into the room above shook the entire building, striking fear into the hearts of the children and women—(already all street lights and electric power were off). We were in total darkness save for a flash light which was turned on when needed.

"The velocity of the wind was still increasing—crash went another window and again the building trembled and rocked. By 2:45 most of the windows in the north side of the house were gone, and the roar of the wind rushing by was like that of Niagara Falls or of a locomotive inside a tunnel.

"The velocity of the wind still increased and the hall wall against which it was striking through the broken windows shook and trembled as the blasts or harder gusts would strike and the pressure hurt our ears badly. The darkness was a smothery blackness, and each moment someone would ask, 'Do you think the building can stand much longer?' Again and again I reassured Ruth and the children that we were perfectly safe, but believing every moment that the walls

Still Doing Business Monday, September 20th, on Miami Beach, Though Not as Usual. The Clippers and Chair Were Saved in This Barber Shop.

could not hold out against that withering, crushing, tearing storm—other buildings were giving way— wreckage was striking our building with such force that the noise of the impacts could be heard above the din and roar of the raging storm, and water driven through the broken windows and every crack and crevice, was trickling down the walls in little streams.

"The pressure on our eardrums was both painful and terrifying—(would daylight only come?). To be crushed in the building or swept into the storm offered little choice—no human could stand against the fury of the onward rush of wind, now over two miles per minute. By 3:30 or 4 o'clock in the morning the vacuum caused by

the terrific speed of the wind past the front of the building had pulled the front door partly past the jams and with a rope tied to the inside knob three of us were required to keep it from being pulled and torn out entirely—another two hours would bring daylight—it seemed it would never come—seconds seemed hours, hours an eternity. It was five o'clock when we could feel relief—the roar of the storm was dying down some, and at six o'clock dawn began to break through, six-thirty daylight—most welcome I had ever seen—seven o'clock calm. The strain had told on mothers and babies—white drawn faces and tear stains—giving way to smiles, the wind died down completely, it was almost

View of South Miami Beach Immediately After the Storm and Ocean Waters Had Subsided.

dead calm, there was only a light breeze during the lull, for a lull it proved to be.

"The WIOD radia towers in front of our building were broken down—the roofs were off many houses—the Sisters of St. Dominick's dormitory building in which they were living was still standing, but roof partly off —(they are safe)—the furniture and beds in the apartments on the north side are drenched. We tried to sweep out the water—save the bedding and clothes and survey the premises—we were thankful for our lives—we wondered about others. Wires, trees, awnings, roofs, furniture scattered everywhere was evidence of the havoc wrought—lives must have been lost. How will we feed the babies—the electricity and water are off—the wind had now changed from the north to the south. Is the storm coming back? It is back—it is on us now—why didn't we get the Sisters out of their building? We rushed to lock every window on the south side of the building, closed the fire doors again (it may not be bad). By 8:30 the wind had again reached 90 to 100 miles—9:00 o'clock it is growing steadily worse. Ten o'clock a crash and strange roar, more terrifying than ever before—we cannot see out ten feet, the rain is like a white sheet. Is it rain?—no! the water is already three feet deep.

"The ocean is on us—higher and higher—two feet—three feet—four-foot waves driven by the wind and sheets of white spray. That pain in our ears again, the building trembled and rocked. The water is at the floor in the hall—the wind over 150 miles per hour—the roar is louder—crash—boom—crash, boom—nothing can withstand this—we are gone. In resignation—suspense and lightning-like reflection I thought the Sisters' building must be gone this time. The babies began crying—they don't know the sea is all around us. We wait—our hearts pound, we cannot hide our anxiety now. Maybe the water will not rise any higher. The windows are all gone long ago. Rain and spray are beating in—sheets of spray are on every side. Eleven o'clock, the worst is over, the water is being driven into the bay—we are saved and spared again.

"Out of the din and roar of the storm a man staggered to the front door—he shouted—'Are the Sisters

A Bread Line at Miami Beach For the Benefit of Refugees and Voluntary Helpers, Monday, September 20th, 1926.

here? No?' that was all he could say—he was groping his way through water waist deep to the building where they were living. The roof was gone—the side was gone. Getting into bathing suits three of us followed to help him. The Sisters were huddled into a small hall, drenched and weeping—saved by the lower walls standing. Father Barry had started out from the Spanish Village, at 15th street, Miami Beach, during the lull between the storms in a bathing suit, and after three and one-half hours battling his way two miles through wind and waves arrived to find they were safe, but all the school buildings wrecked and in ruins. At five o'clock Saturday evening I went with Father Barry to try to get some food, if possible, for the

eighteen people now in our building.

"The sight of torn and bleeding Miami Beach that greeted us was enough to break the spirit and heart of a battle-scarred soldier. People moved about with only one thought—food, water—sleep. Realization of losses did not occur. The dead are to be buried, the injured cared for, and sleep and rest needed to restore sanity and ability to think.

"We all slept, eighteen (18) of us, in two three-room apartments Saturday night on wet bedding, and are now cooking food on one oil stove, eating community style at a large table fixed in one of the water-soaked rooms until it is possible to make a survey of the conditions of the Beach and of the City of Miami. We

Alton Road, Miami Beach, as It Appeared Before the Light Poles Had Been Straightened, But After Trees Had Been Cleared Away.

The Remains of the Warehouse at the Meteor Docks, Miami Beach, After the Storm.

Wreckage on County Causeway in Front of Power House Showing Bridge to Star Island in the Distance. This Causeway was Impassible for Several Days After Storm of Sept. 17 and 18, 1926.

cannot get to Miami on account of the causeways, one of which is wrecked badly.

"So finding ourselves situated as we are, with every line of communication broken, a great many of us realize, probably for the first time in our lives, what a real brotherhood of man means, and how unimportant we really are, and I think that before we are able to get back to living alone again that many things which we would not have considered doing three days ago, we shall be glad to do without a murmur of complaint. Nothing is of much importance except our lives, and losses that have been sustained by the different ones in the apartments, are not even mentioned nor considered, and everyone appears to be anxious to serve everyone else and try to make them comfortable under present existing conditions. I will write again in the next few days and tell you in detail how we get along and meet the situation which confronts us.

"Assure all of our friends and relatives of our safety, as I haven't time to write more now."

Chief R. H. Woods, of the Miami Beach police, is one of the outstanding heroes of the storm. While inspecting damage on the county causeway, he observed a woman clinging to the concrete railing of the bridge at the causeway's eastern end. By this time the swirling waters of the Bay were three feet deep over the causeway pavement. He crawled on his hands and knees with the frightful wind roaring from the southeast and caught her hand as it was slipping. Excitement and nature brought about the immediate birth of a child. Chief Woods assisted and then fought his way with the invalid and baby against the howling storm and rushing brine five hundred yards to the Floridian Hotel where

mother and child are "doing nicely" today.

Ice is being issued to families with babies only —and it is very warm today. More than 200 men are repairing the power and light wires. Almost every light wire on Miami Beach was blown down and nearly all transformers were destroyed. They are trying to repair the county causeway. The Red Cross is making a canvass of the Beach to relieve any sufferer unable to get to the Floridian Hotel or Allison Hospital. Permits must be gotten for the purchase of food and the City of Miami Beach has made a special emergency appropriation of $10,000 to care for those unable to purchase food because of temporary absence of cash.

View of County Causeway Showing 9,000-Ton Dredge in the Background. At the Left is Part of the Street Car Tracks Which Were Washed Entirely Out, Together With All Poles Carrying Trolleys. Palm Island Home Can Be Seen at Extreme Upper Left.

It is reported the bodies of Jerome Cherbino and his wife have been found two miles from their home at Golden Beach which was demolished. Mr. Cherbino was builder and owner of the Floridian Hotel and both he and Mrs. Cherbino were social leaders on Miami Beach.

Another rumor has it that 120 negroes and 35 white men working on S. A. Lynch's development at Sunny Isles, five miles north of Miami Beach, are all dead except four white men.

Commodore Stoltz's Fleetwood Hotel, home of yachtsmen, escaped with slight damage to its lobby and ground floor.

It is growing dark. There are no lights. We were ordered to return across the causeway before dark. Collins Avenue, as we drive north again to Lincoln Road, is shrouded in gloom. We are challenged at every corner by the military and special police. Only three cars on Collins Avenue for fifteen blocks. Sidewalks are deserted. Regulations say everyone must be inside by six o'clock unless armed with a pass.

As we cross the causeway the sky-line of Miami looms dimly against the darkling sky, lightless and gaunt, like the ghost of a metropolis.

Miami Beach's troubles are shown by the following official bulletin published Tuesday:

The City of Miami Beach will have their censor stationed at the West end of the Venetian Causeway and the West end of that causeway will be policed by either the sheriff's department or the Miami police department and ALL cars will be allowed to pass after they receive the sanction of the Miami Beach censor.

The old (County) causeway will be CLOSED TO THE PUBLIC at both ends with the exception of construction gangs repairing the viaduct and the automobiles of residents on the several islands connected with the mainland by way of this bridge. Traffic over the old causeway from Palm Island either East or West will be under direction of the Miami Beach police department.

The repairing of both causeways and a desire on the part of all municipal and county departments to rebuild homes and business houses, clear debris and keep undesirables from both cities makes this order imperative.

HENRY CHASE, *Sheriff of Dade County.*
C. A. RENSHAW, *City Manager, Miami Beach.*
POLICE CHIEF R. H. WOODS, *Miami Beach.*
LIEUT. W. J. MCCARTHY *for Chief Quigg, Miami.*
COUNCILMAN C. B. FLOYD, *Miami Beach.*
COUNCILMAN J. NEWTON LUMMUS, *Miami Beach.*
COUNCILMAN F. H. HENNING, *Miami Beach.*

Police Chief R. H. Woods, One of Miami Beach's Heroes of September 17th and 18th, 1926.

Mayor Snedigar of Miami Beach.

J. S. Stephenson, Safety Director of Miami Beach.

Editorial from *Miami Daily News* of Monday, printed in the plant of the *Miami Herald*, first newspaper to receive electric power:

THE WILL TO DO
(Editorial)

San Francisco was levelled by an earthquake; and she came back stronger than ever.

Galveston was swept by a tidal wave; and she came back stronger than ever.

It was not circumstances, but men which accomplished these results. Miami has been devastated by a hurricane.

She will come back stronger than ever.

Because she has the men; men of indomitable courage; men who can look disaster in the face and say, "Thank God, it could have been worse"; because

she has the men with the will to do; men who do not know when to quit.

So, today, with wreckage all about us, Miami grits her teeth and gets down to the serious business of rehabilitation.

We are determined to make Miami a greater Miami than it was, and a better Miami than we had hoped it would be.

Pessimism is routed from the city. Optimism, born of the will to do, reigns.

REALIZATION of sufferings in the Florida storm zone was borne down by the Nation's Chief Executive who gave impetus to relief work throughout the country by the following message to the American people:

Washington, Sept. 20.—(By the Associated Press.)— President Coolidge today appealed to the American people to come to the assistance of sufferers in the Florida disaster.

The President's proclamation follows:

"An overwhelming disaster has come to the people of Miami, Hollywood and surrounding communities in Southern Florida. Such assistance as is within the means of the executive department of the government will be rendered, but, realizing the great suffering which now needs relief and will need relief for days to come, I am prompted to appeal urgently to the American people, whose sympathies have always been so comprehensive, to contribute generously in aiding the sufferers of this disaster.

"That the utmost co-ordination and effectiveness in the administration of the relief funds may be obtained, I urge that all contributions for this purpose be sent to the American National Red Cross at Washington or to the local Red Cross chapters."

MONDAY MIDNIGHT, SEPTEMBER 20:

WE HAVE just looked at 64 corpses stark and still in three undertaking parlors. We were searching for missing persons. Those identified have baggage tags attached by wire to their ankles. Bodies are laid for lack of space on the floors of offices, embalming rooms and garages. The dead range in age from children of 15 months to old men and women of 70 years and over. Few were mangled. Here's a body of a beautiful blonde girl, about 19 years old. Not a scratch. Not a broken bone. She looks to be sleeping. Must have died of fright. Over here a mother and two children are crowded onto the same slab.

The McAllister Hotel, Emergency Hospital. Columbus Hotel Adjoining on the Right.

The Florida Hurricane
America's Greatest Storm

CHAPTER FOUR

Ice is scarce and the odor is stifling. We asked whether the body of a certain man had been brought in. The answer: "Can't say. Go on out and look 'em over. We brought in an old fellow about ten minutes ago out of the Bay. Oh, Charley, where did you leave that old boy? You don't know! Charley is a little cuckoo. He's been going for 36 hours. Take these men out there, Charley, and look in the garage behind the cars. He's there somewhere. If they keep hauling them in we'll have to lay 'em on the roof, and we have no roof."

The McAllister Hotel could be a base hospital behind the lines in France. Marines guard the entrances from Flagler Street and Biscayne Boulevard. Ambulances — dozens of them — take their turn at backing up to the curb and unloading their burdens of suffering survivors. Every now and then a stretcher is brought out bearing the form of someone who could hold out no longer. Doctors and nurses have been on their feet since Saturday noon. Other physicians

Northeast Second Avenue With Wreckage as it Appeared Saturday Evening, September 18th, Showing Emergency Relief Cars in Service of the Red Cross.

with nurses and supplies are arriving from Jacksonville, Daytona Beach, Orlando and West Palm Beach. Met Dr. Davis Forster of New Smyrna.

A children's nursery and emergency hospital is being organized in the White Temple by the Juvenile Court through the Big Brothers Federation, in charge of Major W. S. Nicholson, chief probation officer, and Dr. Johnson of the Red Cross. Preparations are being made to care for

two hundred children whose parents are missing.

Ten babies were born in the various hospitals since the storm. 174 premature births occurred in the Miami district.

The food committee has been vested with full authority under martial law and has been instructed by Frank H. Wharton, City Manager, to seize any food supplies that may be necessary and to close or take over the operation of any

food selling establishment where evidence of profiteering is shown.

Two men were reported shot early tonight while looting. The military and special police have orders to shoot to kill.

The city is in darkness except for the McAllister Hotel and the offices of the *Miami Herald* to which the Florida Power & Light Company managed to lay one wire, having placed transformers on a truck in the street.

Groups of weeping men and women walk through the dark, gloomy streets from one hospital and nursery to another searching for missing relatives.

The Everglades Hotel, operated by the Fred F. French Company, at Biscayne Boulevard and Third Street, is taking in all who come and asking no questions. It is full to the 17th floor and apartment holders are now doubling up with strangers.

Governor John W. Martin has ordered the Tampa unit of the 116th Field Artillery to entrain at once for Miami. They are bringing 1,000 beds and a carload of food supplies. Tampa was struck by the fringe of the storm, but sustained damage of only $100,000. There were no deaths despite the fact that waters of Tampa Bay and the Hillsboro river washed high over the banks.

Hundreds of Boy Scouts are aiding in relief work, escorting ambulances and nurses, directing traffic and running messages. Roy Narcato, 15, of Lemon City, member of Troop No. 24, was continuously on duty as orderly and messenger boy from one o'clock this morning to seven o'clock this evening, 18 hours. He will receive a certificate of merit.

Messages of sympathy are pouring in over one

Naval Reserves for Guard Duty in the Devastated Area.

rehabilitated wire from cities throughout the United States, Canada, Mexico, England and France. Among the American and Canadian cities heard from today are Galveston, Sacramento, San Francisco, Los Angeles, Nashville, Louisville, Minneapolis, Savannah, Richmond, Atlanta, Cincinnati, Brooklyn, South Bend, Tampa, Asheville, Seattle, Montreal, Victoria, B. C., and Winnipeg.

Ten special trains are rushing to us from the outside world. The *Herald-Examiner* of Chicago is sending a train carrying physicians, nurses, antitoxin, food and milk.

A typhoid scare has broken out. Health authorities are using every possible means to warn people to boil all drinking water and disinfect refuse. City water is off and sanitary conditions are extremely bad in the large hotels. Men are carrying pails of water as high as 17 floors to flush toilets. Typhus and tetanus vaccination is being given free at all hospitals and medical stations.

Special attention is being given sanitary conditions in the negro district where some 20,000 blacks live in a congested area of about a hundred square blocks. This section of the city escaped with slight damage owing to the fact that the homes were mostly of frame construction and one story and built close together.

Four hundred men are replacing the telephone and telegraph wires between Miami and West Palm Beach which are down the entire distance.

A full moon beams down tonight on devasted Miami. It throws across Biscayne Bay a wide sheen of silver. Balmy zephyrs out of the southeast fan the face like wings of ministering angels. Miami is a temperamental woman. After her storms come long periods of gentle tropical wooing.

K. of C. Relief, One of the Many Organizations Which Distributed Supplies to Victims of the Florida Disaster.

The Steamer "Jacksonville," Whose Decks Were Swept by the Hurricane, as She Appeared in Biscayne Bay on the Evening of Sept. 21st, 1926.

The Spirit of Miami is Portrayed by This Picture Taken on September 21, 1926. Many signs of This Kind Were in Evidence Throughout the Stricken Area.

Mute Evidence of the Havoc Wrought by the Turbulent Waters Are to Be Seen in This Picture of the County Causeway, Between Miami and Miami Beach. Fleetwood and Floridian Hotels in Distance. Florida Light and Power Plant Extreme Right.

Miami's Spirit Rises Above the Ruins.

IN THE absence of Mayor E. C. Romfh, James H. Gilman, acting mayor, assigned the various relief and reconstruction departments in the following official bulletin:

OFFICIAL BULLETIN

Railroad and Steamship
 Transportation ....NORMAN GRAVES
Unskilled Labor ....CECIL WATSON
Gas, Oil, Fuel.........................H. O. SHAW
Shelter and Housing...........JOHN MacDONOUGH
Burial and Mortuary ....J. J. COMBS

American Legion ....R. V. WATERS, COL. DUNCAN
Acting Vice Commander Boy Scouts..........NORSK
Chamber of Commerce.................L. W. CROW
Publicity and Information..............F. L. WEEDE
Home Reconstruction ....McGEE
Interdepartmental Organization ......S. P. ROBINEAU
Salvation Army ....MAJ. D. McMILLAN

MR. TELFAIR KNIGHT, *of Coral Gables, and* MR. C. B. FLOYD, *of Miami Beach, are cooperating with all departments.*

The operation of all these departments is coordinated into an Interdepartmental Bureau, with headquarters at the County Court House, in the offices of the Clerk of the Circuit Court. The temporary addresses of headquarters of all these departments may be obtained at the Interdepartmental Bureau. The permanent location of these departments will be announced as soon as the proper location can be procured. In the meanwhile the Bureau offices at the Court House will furnish necessary means for acquiring relief to all applicants. However, it is requested that all applicants for relief apply to the particular department covering the service sought, if it is possible.

The circulation of all pedestrian and vehicular traffic is permitted in all parts of Miami, for necessary purposes; the public is earnestly requested to desist from idle sightseeing and traveling on the highways for at least the next few days. Persons in pursuit of a useful object will be helped on their way, but do not abuse the privilege. This, however, applies only to the daylight hours. After sunset all travel and circulation not directly in connection with the work of one of the departments is forbidden. Passes will be issued to all actually engaged in any department's activities.

The passage to and from Miami Beach is restricted to work in connection with general relief and urgent individual needs. The causeways must be kept as open as possible for the transportation of food and supplies. Idle circulation of pedestrians and vehicles retards the progress of vitally important transportation and the expedition of repairs.

There are sufficient supplies of food and building materials. Labor has generously offered its services to the authorities for the effectuation of immediate reconstruction of the houses of the poor. Plans are now being formulated to restore the homes of the destitute. Make known your honest needs to the several departments and the committee will do its utmost to provide you necessaries.

Every energy is being expended to make water, lights, gas and power available to all. These public utilities are already in full operation in several parts of the city, and the other parts will be supplied as soon as it is physically possible. Everything that can be done is being done, and no detail is being omitted.

All people are warned to exercise every care in the disposal of garbage and personal sewage, especially where the plumbing and water supply are defective. We recommend that every individual apply immediately to the medical service upon feeling any symptoms of illness, so that contagious diseases may be averted at the outset. The street cleaning is progressing very rapidly and it is hoped that streets will be covered in a very few days. A bacteriologist is at work analyzing all water supplies to control contamination and contagion. All water from doubtful sources should be boiled.

Every possible precaution is being taken by the authorities to restore order and comfort. With the hearty cooperation of all persons, the efforts of the officials and the committees and departments, Miami will be restored to comparative normalcy in a very short time.

CITY OF MIAMI,
JAMES H. GILMAN, *Acting Mayor.*

"Miami Is Master of Her Fate"

The *Miami Tribune* of Tuesday had the following to say anent relief work and reconstruction:

MIAMI IS MASTER OF HER FATE

"It matters not how strait the gate,
How filled with punishment the scroll,
I am the Master of my fate,
I am the captain of my soul."

———

Miami, quivering like a broken reed after the gale has passed, has assumed charge of her own fate. She has asked for and accepted the aid of soldiers to maintain order, a martial law to protect such property as she has left. She has accepted gifts of bread, ice and milk.

She is accepting tents, cots, bedding and clothing to a limited amount. She has refused the offers of some other forms of aid from the outside world, and now, as this is written in West Palm Beach, there are rumors afloat that Miami is too haughty to accept needed aid.

Far from that, she is humbled by the storm. Relief funds are being formed. Relief supplies of staple foodstuffs are needed for the future but they are not needed today. There are some few Miamians who are suffering for food, but that is because of the impossibility of getting it to them.

Miamians wisely have acted to prevent a stampede of supplies into Miami, supplies which would necessarily be wasted today, but which may be sorely needed the day after tomorrow. To permit the wholesale waste of supplies tendered by well-meaning friends would

be a disgrace to the city, and a black mark against her integrity. She will accept only such things as she actually wants for.

Ice, milk, water and bread are the most important of these.

As this is written, The Palm Beach Times has a fund of more than $600 donated by the citizens of West Palm Beach. It will be turned over, at the proper time, to such organizations as are in authority at Miami and Hollywood, organizations who are in a position to know how to spend it most wisely.

Other funds are being raised all over the country, and the funds will be available to aid Miami. They will not be permitted to waste. The real friends of Miami will not feel piqued if offers of aid are rejected temporarily by those in charge, those who see that acceptance would be waste rather than a frank statement of conditions.

Leading Miami grocers say there is food enough in Miami to last for two weeks. Trains are running and boats will be, by which more can be brought. Ice will help save such perishable food as is there.

Miami is preparing to rebuild her city and care for her tourist population when it comes this winter. She has work to do. Work is her real need. Her own citizens can do a large part of it. If they can be fed, housed and clothed for a short time, they will be able to clean their city up, to rebuild their damaged structures, and to face the future with confidence.

Miami is master of its own fate, to change the pronoun's gender. Out of its tribulation it will spring Venus-like a full-fledged city from the brow of adversity, though its suffering is terrible.

Start of Reconstruction in a Little River Garage.

TUESDAY, SEPTEMBER 21:

Miami is fighting back today. A semblance of order has risen out of the chaos of the last three days, and the excitement and hysteria that have reigned since the hurricane are giving place to sober realization of our plight and united effort towards rehabilitation.

Contact with the outside was aided today when the Tropical Radio station at Hialeah strung a

The Florida Hurricane
America's Greatest Storm

CHAPTER FIVE

temporary line to the power plant north of Opa-Locka. The five steel towers supporting the antennæ are a mass of wreckage. Four of them were 439 feet high and the fifth was 460 feet high. Six members of the crew narrowly escaped death when the hurricane twisted the great steel towers to the earth with a deafening crash.

Henry Baker, National Disaster Director of the American Red Cross, arrived by airplane today and is conferring with the Citizens' Committee, headed by Frank B. Shutts. Mr. Baker narrowly escaped death in making the air trip here. The machine crashed into an Alabama swamp and was demolished, but he and the pilot escaped with minor bruises.

Governor John W. Martin came to the city this morning, and is taking a directing hand in relief work and reconstruction. While the State's Chief Executive was in Miami the *Daily News* printed on its front page the following blast, which attitude roused so much support here that the city's call for national aid is receiving much opposition. Under the heading "Florida Should Help Herself," the *Daily News* said:

Florida is being placed in a bad light throughout the country when there is no excuse for this condition.

With a state treasury bulging with unexpended balances—the greatest balance in the treasury of any state of the Union—Gov. John W. Martin is permitting appeals to be broadcast throughout the nation for financial assistance when Florida is well able to take care of her own.

It is five days now since the hurricane centered on Dade county and then passed northwestward over the state, doing incalculable damage to property and taking a toll of life that it is not now possible to determine with accuracy.

Only the north central and northeastern sections of the state escaped the wrath of the storm. It left its marks on the richest areas, agriculturally and industrially. It left many dead, thousands homeless and thousands of injured in its wake.

The need for medical assistance was urgent. That was forthcoming from every section of the country. For this assistance, Florida—and Dade county in particular—is more grateful than it is possible to express in words. Without it, we might have suffered more than we have.

Now, order has been restored, the food supply is

Coconut Grove Sep 18 1926

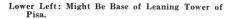

Coconut Grove · Remains After Hurricane Sep 18-1926

Upper Left: Coconut Grove Home Shivered by the Blast. Small House at Left is a Houseboat.

Upper Right: Concrete Block House at Coconut Grove Collapsed Like a Toy Home.

Lower Left: Might Be Base of Leaning Tower of Pisa.

Lower Right: Ruins of Motion Picture Studio in Hialeah.

WILLY WILLYS INN

Center: The Seminole Indian Villages Wiped Out. This Village Was a Familiar Sight to Visitors and Tourists, Being Located on Palm Avenue, the Main Street in Hialeah.

MOVIE STUDIO HIALEAH AFTER STORM SEPT 18-1926

Clearing Debris in Biscayne Jai-Alai Fronton, Hialeah.

brought the following Miami and Miami Beach business men: Mayor E. C. Romfh, James A. Allison, John H. Levy, Frank B. Shutts, James Fowler and Mr. and Mrs. Jesse Andrews.

Messages of sympathy and offers of assistance are pouring in from all sections of the country. Mayor James Rolph, Jr., of San Francisco, has wired as follows: "In the name of all our citizens, I extend to you and to the people of Miami our heartfelt sympathy in the disaster which has stricken your beautiful city. We of San Francisco realize what this means because of the distressing experience that we ourselves went through in 1906. While we are doubtless too widely separated to permit the sending of relief in the way of food and other necessities, we nevertheless wish to help you recover from this calamity and stand willing to do all we can in whatever way you suggest. Please advise me how best we may be of service. Sincerest good wishes for Miami's early rehabilitation."

Commander Evangeline Booth, of the Salvation Army, wired from New York City:

"My heart goes out in profound sympathy to you and your citizens and to the people of the surrounding communities. However it is our desire as an organization to give our sympathy practical expression in terms of immediate and effective aid. Our forces in Florida are already mobilized and on the ground for emergency relief activity and all resources as an organization are at your disposal. Let me know of any further service you might wish us to perform."

Other messages were sent from Dallas, El Paso, Detroit, Tallahassee and Richmond, the last named sending by airplane 280,000 units of tetanus anti-toxin.

assured, disease preventive measures have been taken and the civil government is functioning as it should.

The next step is rehabilitation.

That is a task where the aid of the state government is essential and imperative.

That aid should be forthcoming immediately.

Governor Martin should call a special session of the legislature at once to take what action, in its judgment, is wise and advisable. There should be no hemming or hawing about this. The public welfare demands action and speedy action.

Governor Martin made public the statement that the city was *not* under martial law, and that he had never made such an order. The troops, however, will remain here to act as auxiliaries to the county and city officials.

A record run from New York was made yesterday, by a special train chartered by Joseph W. Young, founder and developer of Hollywood. Leaving New York at 10 o'clock Monday morning it made the run to Miami in 31 hours and

Jerome Cherbino and Mrs. Cherbino, of Miami Beach, are alive. It has been found Mr. Cherbino was in New York at the time of the storm and Mrs. Cherbino had stayed with friends on the Beach. Al Little, advertising manager of the *Miami Beach Beacon*, was killed Saturday morning when a section of the ceiling of the Wofford Hotel fell on him and Kent Watson. It is reported today Stan Comstock, recently named in connection with a threatened marriage to Peggy Hopkins Joyce, is dead with his wife. They were last seen on their yacht, the Don C., heading for the Florida Keys.

This morning I went to see Brickell Avenue, Coconut Grove, Larkins and South Miami. South Florida's oldest and most aristocratic residential districts along Biscayne Bay are devastated almost beyond recognition. The morning storm of Saturday swept the waters of the Bay over the water-front line of elegent residences from the Miami River to the southern section of Coconut Grove. Wind and water spent their titanic force on these charming estates and left them mere shells of their former grandeur. Brickell Avenue resembles a treed street in Ontario in autumn. Branches of the once heavily foliaged trees now sway in the breeze like so many sticks. Not a royal palm could be found standing along the residential bay-front. All private piers are gone and every exposed yacht was sunk. The entire street that curved gracefully around Point View is crumbled wreckage and at this point more than any other the homes seem to have suffered almost irremediable damage. Rushing waters inundated the ground floor of the Frank B. Shutts home, destroyed every tree in the yard, and did damage to thousands of dollars to the

The Remains of a Home in South Miami.

costly furniture. Farther south along Brickell Avenue the homes of Mrs. Emily J. Clarke and Mrs. Bernard Gimbel, of New York, sustained damage that will require months to repair. Villa Serena, former home of William Jennings Bryan, took the brunt of the hurricane on its southeastern exposure. The vast yard with its variety of tropical foliage is desolate. Outer masonry along the bay, the ground floor of the house, and the furniture are almost completely useless.

The famous estate of James Deering presents one of the most eloquent bits of testimony to the storm's force. It was one of America's most magnificent estates built up over a period of ten years, at a cost to the harvester magnate of $15,000,000. Dense foliage which formerly hid the great mansion and sunken gardens from view has been stripped bare and laid low. Costly pieces of statuary brought from the galleries of Europe by Mr. Deering, an ardent lover of art, lie face down and broken on the ground whither they were hurled from their pedestals by the rush of the winds. Every royal palm on the stately avenue over the bridge south of the Venetian Villa is prostrate and shorn of its leaves. Though the villa itself stood out against the gale by sheer strength of its masonry, the statuary bordering the sunken gardens is shattered in many places and the famous labyrinth, wherein the wealthy owner was wont to amuse his many guests in eccentric fashion, is a mass of tumbled debris. The mansion itself sustained little damage, but the wide flag stones in front, between the residence and the Bay, are undermined. The boat house still stands.

The Deering gardens, hot houses and spacious servant quarters west of Brickell Avenue escaped with slight damage, protected as they were by the tall Spanish wall that lines the estate along the street.

The main highway through Coconut Grove, pronounced by the late President Harding the most beautiful in the United States, cannot until some future day again take its position as such. Hundreds of graceful Australian pines, whose drooping branches formed a canopy of passing beauty, now lie across the road. Those that withstood the storm are shorn of their foliage and stand naked and gaunt. The luxurious estates of Miami's elite along the Bay Front present a sorry spectacle with their yawning window frames, wrecked verandas and water logged furniture. Here in Coconut Grove foregathered the scholars of South Florida and their thousands of friends from northern circles of art, literature, music, science and education, who come to Miami every winter. The clans of learning will gather once more this coming season in Coconut Grove, for the mind needs not elegant surrounding for its exercise; and today many mentalities with artistic and literary penchants are directed towards shoveling fallen plaster and drying out rugs.

The Open-Air Church of Coconut Grove was damaged only slightly and — one of the miracles of the storm—the matted bougainvilea still adorns its rustic walls.

Larkins, which now is South Miami, suffered experiences similar to its sister suburbs. Many buildings were completely demolished and havoc was wrought among the large fruit warehouses along the tracks of the Florida East Coast Railway. Returning to the city by way of Red Road to the Tamiami Trail I was impressed by the fact that Coral Gables homes escaped damage more than any section in the path of the hurricane. After visiting the ruins of my home on Murcia Avenue and noting a sickening feeling at the pit of my stomach as I viewed the totally destroyed furniture, I made the rounds of Coral Gables. Except for a portion of the servants' quarters of the Miami-Biltmore giving way before the storm, the great structure was intact and was now housing several hundred residents of Coral Gables until their homes could be made habitable. George Merrick and Telfair Knight told me the damage to Coral Gables would not exceed $1,500,000, divided three ways between the city, the Coral Gables Corporation and the thousands of property owners. "Doc." Dammers, mayor of Coral Gables, is reported as saying that only three homes in Central Miami were damaged. The Coral Gables administration building escaped with broken windows and some water-soaked furnishings, and the Venetian Pools sustained minor damage to the interior. But part of the business district was laid waste.

It is confined in a square bounded by Ponce de Leon Boulevard, Coral Way, LeJeune Road and Alcazar Avenue. Several structures in this square were razed, including a printing and supply building of the corporation, a garage and some stores. The Construction Building was unharmed, but the Ground Sales office got some pretty rough treatment on its lower floor. Most of the exterior damage to Coral Gables was in the destruction of trees and the uprooting of shrubbery. Not a grapefruit remains, but the trees can all be brought back in a few months.

Fulford up to today has a death list of nine, with twenty-five injured. Hardly a house stands roofed, or with walls intact owing to falling trees. Towers of Radio Station WGBU were bent downward from the 50-foot level. The old Fulford Administration Building in Central Park and the dance casino were demolished. The giant automobile speedway, on which the world's fastest drivers raced last New Year's Day, was spread over several dozen city blocks and only half the track remains. The three grandstands built to seat 20,000 were completely demolished. All power and light wires are down and it will be at least a month before residents of Fulford will enjoy these utilities. Although built to the very edge of the ocean, the Sunny Isles Casino withstood the hurricane.

Relief is pouring in. Two hours after President Coolidge issued his call to the American people to aid South Florida more than $500,000 had been subscribed, it was made known by radio tonight. The American Red Cross has set its mark at $5,000,000 for relief in the devastated districts of this State.

The dead in the Miami District up to tonight

Center: This was a Miami Home.

Upper Left: Devastation in Royal Palm Park.

Upper Right: Two-Masted Schooners Aground in Heart of City of Miami.

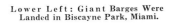

Lower Left: Giant Barges Were Landed in Biscayne Park, Miami.

Lower Right: Freight Cars Turned Over Close to Docks, Bay Shore Drive, at Sixth Street, Miami.

number 105, according to the official count. There are about 2,000 injured in the various hospitals and approximately 300 persons missing. The list of the dead as of this evening is as follows:

WHITE

Armours, Lawrence	Martin, James
Ayers, Thomas V.	Murphy, John Joseph
Adams, Charles	Murphy, Paul
Bynum, Tullia Hayes	McKenzie, Frank
Brinson, Mrs. Matties	McGinnis, Mrs. Nellie W.
Ballou, Mrs. Amy	McGinnis, Joseph W., Jr.
Baker, Mrs. Edith F.	McGinley, Catherine.
Beum, Carolyn R.	Newton, Harden
Calcutt, Aubrey S.	Petty, John
Carter, Venetion	Rogers, Grady
Conner, John H., Jr.	Rader, Mrs. Martha W.
Cotters, Henry	Rogers, James E.
Cracraft, Margrete	Rexford, Mary
Edwards, John H.	Rexford, Junior
Egan, John J.	Roberts, Victoria
Elvis, Offie T.	Roberts, Tolula A.
Estey, William A.	Shope, Theo. A.
Fisher, Little Don.	Shutts, Fred
Glover, Mrs. Ammer	Smith, Jennie
Godwin, Mary G.	Shucks, Esther
Hamilton, Leroy	Stephens, Lila Mae
Horton, John	Schwartz, Frank
Harris, James T.	Schoenback, Jules
Hultgren, Bruno	Sawyer, Randolph
Haskins, W. J.	Schachter, Isadore
Hoehr, Chris.	Snow, Mrs. Freeman P.
Hargraves, Ralph	Tuley, John A.
Harrison, Mrs. Ella	Thomas, T.
Harrison, A. D.	Walls, Dorothy
Hopper, Mrs. Mary A.	Wall, Mrs. Ethel
Kusta, Edna	Winslow, Hattie M.
Kirbey, Dorothy	Watts, Benjamin F.
Leet, Georgia Mae	Wilkes, Mrs. Dora
Lehman, Tillson K.	Wunnenberg, A. J.
Little, Alton Bush	Whitehurst, Mrs. S. A.
Lowe, Lillie	Woodall, John

NEGROES

Best, Isaiah	Hayes, George
Green, Will	Bain, Ralph
George, "Shorty"	Berrien, Ducilla
Robinson, Meddow	Houston, Sam
McKinney, Arthur	Neal, Harper
McKinney, Leona	Wing, Esther
Washington, George	Brown, Willie
	Sudley, John

In the above list the reader will notice the names of Mrs. Nellie McGinnis and Joseph W. McGinnis, Jr. The elder McGinnis was at work in Lake Worth, near Palm Beach, when the storm broke. After a night of fighting the tirade of the elements for his own life he started in a small car for Miami full of fears for the safety of his little family. The Dixie Highway was impassible because of fallen trees and telegraph poles, but McGinnis, with the fatherly instinct raging in his breast, hacked his way as far as Boca Raton. There he met three Miami newspapermen trying to get to West Palm Beach to send details of the disaster north. They persuaded him to help them with his car. After landing them three hours later in West Palm Beach, he started for Miami, a distance of 72 miles. Arriving there he went to Hialeah and to the site of his former home—for the site was all that remained. He found the humble cottage a heap of ruins and neighbors were forced to tell him that his wife and son were dead and his little daughter, six, in the emergency hospital with a broken leg. This morning one of the newspaper party that McGinnis helped to West Palm Beach met him on the street. "Hello, McGinnis, how's the family?" asked the reporter. "They're gone to Heaven," was the tearful reply.

Thomas Gill, of Hialeah, insists that he is alive. He made this announcement in stentorian tones at his own funeral services today at Combs' undertaking rooms. Gill was working on a dredge in the Bay. The storm caught him asleep but the roaring of the elements woke him; he jumped into the raging waves and swam to shore. After the storm divers went down near the dredge and recovered a body. It was identified by his own shipmates as that of Gill. The funeral service was in progress; the minister was reading the 23d Psalm when Gill walked in and stopped the service.

Predatory inclinations were curbed by the following warning in the *Miami Herald* September 22, 1926:

WARNING TO PROFITEERS.

To All Dealers in Food Supplies:

Anyone found guilty of profiteering in food supplies of any description will be subject to immediate arrest, their places of business closed, licenses revoked, and all food supplies found on the premises confiscated.

Citizens are urged to report any violation of this proclamation to the Mayor's Committee, at the City Hall.

What is meant by profiteering is the exacting of prices in excess of those current on Friday, September 17, 1926.

FRANK H. WHARTON,
City Manager, City of Miami.

Approved:

JAS. H. GILMAN,
Acting Mayor.

To All Peace Officers and Citizens of Dade County, Florida:

The services of the National Guard having been officially and regularly called into active service by the Honorable Judge of Dade County, for the protection of life and property, and said units of the guard having reported for duty, be it now and until this order is rescinded known that MARTIAL LAW is declared in Dade County, Florida, and all persons whomsoever will respect this law and obey such persons as are or hereafter will be duly authorized and empowered to enforce same.

ROBERT N. WARD,
Major, 124th Infantry, F. N. G.,
Commanding.

Damaged Plant of Shackelford Motor Company, Buena Vista.

WEDNESDAY, SEPTEMBER 23:

Five years ago J. W. Young, one of Florida's foremost developers, came from Long Beach, California, with a bank-roll of $4,000.00. Choosing for the scene of his operations a wide sweep of sandy soil between the ocean and the Dixie Highway squarely between Miami and Palm Beach, he hoisted a sign "This Is Hollywood." The town sprouted and grew during the first two years, then sprang into brilliant refulgence during the memorable years of 1924 and 1925. Mr. Young made a fortune. In the year 1924 he paid an income tax on more than $1,000,000.

On Tuesday of this week J. W. Young returned from New York to find his Hollywood, his "baby," prostrate after the worst hurricane in America's history had swirled through it for ten hours. Tears came to his eyes as he wended his way through the debris in Hollywood Boulevard and heard the high, wailing sirens of ambulances rushing the dead and mangled or alive and suffering forms of his friends to the morgues and hospitals.

But the man who had sufficient foresight to establish Hollywood five years ago and build it into a city was undaunted by the ravages of the elements. Going to his magnificent new home, now partly in ruins, he issued a statement calling upon all men to aid in restoration of the city to normalcy and promising to devote his life to making of Hollywood ten times the city it was before. "This is a temporary set-back," said Mr. Young. "It has roused us from a feeling of smug satisfaction and will drive us forward to greater triumphs in the years to come."

I saw Hollywood and Fort Lauderdale this

The Florida Hurricane
America's Greatest Storm

CHAPTER SIX

morning. Taking the West Dixie Highway I passed through the devastation in Buena Vista and Little River, already starting towards reconstruction, I came to the tourist camps. Truly the fate of these huddled families was pathetic. The terrific hurricane swept the camps clean in the first hour of its destructive life, leaving thousands of half-clad men, women and children floundering about in the darkness, whipped, numbed and some of them killed by flying branches, scantling and kitchen utensils. Families were torn apart by the force of the mighty storm and some of them reunited only after 48 hours. Dr. Tuttle, who worked for 36 hours in the tourist camps, immediately following the storm, told me that so hysterical and insane were some of the men and women he could gain no information as to whether they had children or where they were. The houses having been constructed of wood and canvas, the devastation among these people was awful to contemplate. Many families were left penniless, bereft of food, clothing and shelter. The Red Cross paid the tourist camps special attention and within 48 hours most of the inhabitants were housed throughout the city.

The Embassy Club at 52nd Street and the Dixie Highway, scene of many an all-night revel, escaped with only broken windows and a portion of the roof whipped off. Farther out, just across the Broward County line, the famous Dixie Club, a frame structure, lost its rear end.

The roof was entirely blown off the Ojus High School. More than 30 modest homes were demolished in this little industrial town. Hallandale suffered the common fate. The tall pines that line the Dixie Highway from Hallandale to Hollywood are 75 per cent gone. But it seems Hollywood proper took the severest brunt of the hurricane. The landscape is splotched with ruined homes. Lunch is being served on many a bare floor, out in the open, under the cerulean skies of Florida. People are laughing and joking amid the wreckage of their homes and children are playing in the ugly piles of shattered tile and stucco. From the Dixie Highway I can count eleven American flags waving over the debris.

Hollywood Boulevard, from the Florida East Coast tracks to the Hollywood Hotel, a distance of two miles, is an avenue of desolation. Office buildings are either lying in the street or completely gutted and their contents strewn over a wide area. The Hollywood Golf and Country Club weathered the blast except for the loss of two end gables, broken windows and ruined furnishings. The loss to this building is placed at $25,000.00.

Before we viewed the storm's work on the Beach we inquired after deaths and injuries.

Hollywood has counted up 56 dead, 350 injured and 86 missing. The hurricane found the city with only one hospital. It was demolished in the first hour of the gale. Four hotels and one school building were then used as temporary relief stations and hospitals. The lack of proper equipment in these buildings was responsible for some of the deaths. More than 800 destitute women and children were carried free Monday

Ruins of Little River Hardware Company.

by the Florida East Coast and Seaboard Air Line railways to points in the north. An order has been issued compelling every citizen to report for inoculation against tetanus and typhoid fever. Meanwhile Caesar La Monaca and his Hollywood Municipal Band plays stirring strains up and down the business district of the city. Were it not for the rushing ambulances and silently moving hearses you might think it was a holiday.

Damage to the great Hollywood Hotel is estimated by Manager Reinhart of the Hollywood Publicity Department at $150,000.00. When the storm warnings arrived Friday afternoon the management piled several tons of cement before the arcade leading under and through the hotel, thinking to keep the ocean waves from inundating the stores and shops. Not only were these like so many match boxes before the tempest but a large portion of the concrete broadwalk in front of the hotel was driven by the gale through the first floor of the hotel. Every single store and shop was gutted so that you would not know stores had been here. Damage to the furnishings of the elaborate lobby was light for it was high above the rushing ocean. The hotel will be open for tourist business on November 15th.

The Hollywood Bathing Casino, scene of nationally known beauty pageants, was almost completely wrecked. The damage is said to be more than $50,000. The Parkview Hotel took a loss of about $40,000, and the Great Southern Hotel some $10,000. Damage to the Hollywood Administration Building is estimated at $20,000. Officials of the Associated Hollywood Companies stated their loss would not exceed $250,000,

covered by insurance. Complete loss figures for the city are placed at between $10,000,000 and $15,000,000.

Chief Tony Tommy, of the Seminole Indians, today told T. Rogers Gore, publisher of the *Hollywood News*, that the hurricane of last Friday and Saturday was the worst in the history of the Seminoles in Florida. This information is not written down but comes by way of tradition handed from one aged man to another. The Chief said that in a storm of 120 years ago no Indians were killed though there were many white victims. He declared Indians are taught from early childhood that when high winds rise they must go into the bushes with blankets wrapped around their bodies and over their face to keep the wind from smothering them and the rain from chilling.

Dania, which is included in the city limits of Hollywood, lies partly in ruins today. Its main street, which is the Dixie Highway, was 50 per cent devastated by the winds, while no home in the city remains totally undamaged. Twenty people met their death in Dania from flying debris and toppling homes. The city has managed to restore light along its main streets and there is sufficient drinking water for all today.

Following is a partial list of the dead at Hollywood, as given out officially today:

Bjorklund, A. P., of Hollywood, age 50, sign painter; part of family at Great Southern Hotel.

Brown, Gordon, of 2227 Grant street, 35, laborer of Enterprise, Ala., buried Hallandale cemetery.

Brown, Mrs. Gordon (Inez), his wife, 28; Hallandale cemetery.

Brown, Murlean, age 4, their daughter; Hallandale cemetery.

Churchill, Edna Allen, of Dania, age 55; Dania cemetery.

Coleman, Roy G., age 27, bookkeeper for Sawyer Motor Co.; buried Dania cemetery.

Corley, Annie, negro, Hollywood, age 42.

Craft, Mrs. J. H., relative of James L. Nickerson, 432 Dania; buried Dania cemetery. No other information.

Crorey, Mrs., of Dania, buried Dania cemetery.

Crorey, Marjory, age 4, Dania, Dania cemetery.

Dwyer, Tom, age 45, timekeeper Hol. Dredging Co., at Bay Mabel.

Frost, Mrs. Sheridan, Dania, age 29; buried Dania cemetery; died of pneumonia.

Frass, George (or Fross), shipped to Indianapolis.

Goodrich, Mrs. Florence, of Hollywood, age 57, employee of Hollywood Publishing Co.

Head, Mrs. Sarah E., Cleveland St. and W. Dixie, 86, from Greenville, S. C.

Helm (or Helms), Mrs. Lorena, age 22, of Dania.

Helm (or Helms), Leon, age 1, Dania cemetery.

Hickman, Miss Nettie, Dania, age 60, Dania cemetery.

Jordan, J. J., Hollywood, age 48, shipped by train to Daleville, Ala.

Luther, Henry Grady, Dania, age 34, Woodlawn cemetery, Dania; brother of S. C. Luther, husband of Mary Ingram Luther; native of Albertville, Ala.

Marshall, George, negro, Hollywood, age 42.

Moore, Mrs. R. W., Dania, Dania cemetery.

Moore, infant, Dania cemetery.

McAllister, John, Dania, age 58, Dania cemetery.

McFarland, Andrew; no information available; see Hollywood Mortuary.

Poole, L. P., Hollywood, age 40, from Hopkinsville, Ky.

Poole, Mrs. L. P., his wife, age 38, Hopkinsville, Ky.

Priess, Mrs. Rhoda Louise, Hollywood Pines, age 55, wife of Julius H.; born St. Albans, Vt.

Rogers, Albert G., Hollywood, age 36, electrical engineer for Florida Power & Light Co.; turned over to King Undertaking Co., Miami; husband of Vivian Rogers; native of Georgia.

Smith, J. R., Hollywood, age 58, carpenter, buried Dania cemetery; born Barton County, Ga.

Terral, James, of Dania.

Vighes, Peter, Dania, box 163, age 50 (approx.), buried Dania cemetery. Effects showed ownership of property in Fort Lauderdale. No other information.

Yeager, Mrs. Effie, Hollywood.

Unidentified man, taken from Park View Hotel, buried Dania cemetery.

A Home in Little River.

Fort Lauderdale, beautiful city on New River, today places the number of its dead at 26, with more than 550 injured and about 160 missing. The business district suffered very severely, some of the city's new skyscrapers being gutted their entire height, but not damaged beyond repair. The Broward Hotel was least damaged of the larger structures. The Chamber of Commerce building has been condemned as dangerous. The Broward County courthouse lost its roof and the Buick agency lacks one of its walls today. The residential district, once among the most beautiful in Florida, met the same fate as that of other cities in the path of the storm. Many charming homes along New River are either totally destroyed or wrecked beyond the possibility of habitation for many weeks. The loss in household goods and furniture cannot be computed. Neither can the loss to boat and yacht owners whose craft was moored for many blocks along the green banks of New River. Fort Lauderdale is known as the yachtsman's paradise. It is one of the famous fishing points in Florida. Many of the yachts sunk in the deep waters of New River are owned by America's foremost sportsmen.

Property loss in Fort Lauderdale, including business blocks, residences, public improvements, yachts and boats, household furniture and store goods, is estimated to be more than $20,000,000.

That tragedy stalked through Broward County's fateful night may be gleaned from some harrowing experiences of citizens of Hollywood and Fort Lauderdale.

A small home in the latter city crashed in early in the storm, pinning its owner under the mass of stucco debris. His wife stood by watching the treacherous waters rising towards the level of the ruins. She made a desperate attempt to free him but her strength had been spent in the losing fight to save the home. Kneeling beside him she held his head as high as possible above the water until almost submerged herself. He pleaded with her to leave him and save herself while there was yet time. Higher rose the lashing water. With a sob she pressed his lips in a last farewell and stumbled away to safety.

The house-boat of Mr. and Mrs. Elmer Crawley of Fort Lauderdale tossed, pitched and finally was capsized, throwing its two occupants into the waters of New River. Crawley snatched up in his arms his wife, who could not swim, and struck out for shore. The raging water forced him back and it was after a terrific struggle that he gained the bank. The storm was now at its height. Mrs. Crawley had fainted—so thought her husband. He lashed her to a tree and went for help. When he returned a few minutes later she was dead.

A young mechanic of Hollywood had worked months to complete a small bungalow into which he brought his bride on the night of Friday, September 17th. That was Florida's night of torture. For hours the young couple battled the elements to save their love nest. The house came in crushing the life out of the young bride of a day. Relief workers next day found the crazed husband with three broken ribs and a fractured arm.

Ted Yates, brother of Colonel B. Y. Yates of Hollywood, was to have been married to a Canadian girl Friday evening of the storm. The bride-to-be was stopping at the Hollywood Hotel, but Ted lived uptown. The storm broke and the seething waters rushed up the boulevard as far as the Dixie Highway, two miles distant. Ted tried at the height of the storm to reach the Hollywood Hotel but was forced back by the relentless hurricane. Next morning, during the lull between storms, he donned his bathing suit and waded to the hotel. She rushed to meet him also in a bathing suit. Their joy in reunion was communicated to the entire hotel staff and a minister was brought in. The young couple were united in matrimony in the lobby of the hotel while Arnold Johnson and his famous orchestra, clad in surf-suits, played the wedding march.

Into what was the small hamlet of Hallandale fourteen years ago, an old couple took in a homeless infant to rear as their own. On the night of the storm Frank, away from the now aged foster parents who had raised him, feared for their safety. Breasting the flood waters he found a small skiff straining at its moorings. Loosing the boat he started out. After hours of struggle through the storm he reached the cottage now all but submerged. After hours of battle with the raging storm he landed the old people to a port of refuge.

"Georgia Boy," a negro lad, was one of Hollywood's characters. Everybody laughed at his antics. They thought he was a little "balmy," and perhaps he was. But on Friday night when the ripping storm was tossing about the dredge on which "Georgia Boy" and four white men had been working, the negro lad fought with the storm to help the "White folks." His white friends lived. They found the body of "Georgia Boy" yesterday.

A woman living in an apartment on the fourth floor at Fort Lauderdale tied a towel about the

Theater Building Miami Shores

What Remained of the Theater at Miami Shores.

cage of her canary Friday evening. This was her nightly way of telling him his singing duties were over for the day. After the storm had subsided and she had fled to safer quarters, she returned to ascertain the extent of damage to her home. About 150 yards from the house she saw the bird cage suspended from the limb of a tree. Releasing it she removed the towel and found dicky bird twittering in all his glory without having lost one small feather.

WEDNESDAY EVENING, SEPTEMBER 22:

White busses that one year ago careened along the paved highways of South Florida bearing tourists, investors and new citizens into Holly-wood-by-the-Sea, today carried refugees of the storm to West Palm Beach, where the Florida East Coast and Seaboard Airline Railways are receiving and sending them, free of charge, to their northern homes.

Gone now the spirit of adventure and excitement, that marked these faces during the days of the "great boom." In their stead tears, discouragement and the wistful expression of homesickness. Tired women in bedraggled clothing alighted with puzzled children from the busses and slowly walked into the station where agents of the railroad companies and Red Cross workers distributed tickets and took down on official writing pads details of suffering and destitution in each case.

More than one thousand refugees from Holly-wood, Dania and Fort Lauderdale were congregated at the West Palm Beach stations on the two days following the hurricane. The few men in the forlorn crowd were either aged or injured. The able-bodied had remained behind for the work of reconstruction.

Red Cross nurses, Boy Scouts and Legionnaires distributed ice water, food and milk to the sufferers. The sight was more striking than that of war. Mothers with infants huddled to their breasts sat prone on the wooden floor of the station or on abutments of the outer masonry of the building.

A train of eleven coaches slowly drew into the station. There was no rush to board the train, just a slow, steady movement of fatigued human beings, who dropped exhausted on the cushions, with a sigh and a gleam of hope in their eyes. They were going home.

The Florida sun was setting. An old man sitting alone at the rear of a coach began to pray aloud. Outside a band was playing "Valencia." Nurses and doctors on the platform stood silent as the train slowly pulled out of the station for the north, a few minutes past nine o'clock.

At Miami it was the same. The station of the Florida East Coast Railway resembled a scene in Belgium before the invaders came. Hundreds of tired people, broken in spirit and without funds, milled about the platform. Many of them were led in a daze to the coaches by relief workers. Others were jolly. Most were silent. There was no cheering as the long train started on its way. Just tears and here and there a little laughter.

South Florida can never forget the yeoman service tendered people of the stricken area by the Florida East Coast and Seaboard Airline Railways.

Perhaps the spirit of Henry M. Flagler, hovering over the scene, whispered to itself: "Help those who followed me, oh God!"

Richard H. Edmonds has been a winter resident of Daytona Beach, Florida, for many years. Wiring to the *Fort Lauderdale News*, Mr. Edmonds says:

MANUFACTURERS RECORD
EXPONENT OF AMERICA
Baltimore, September 21, 1926.

———

To Florida Readers of the Manufacturers Record:

It is with profound sorrow and sympathy that the news of the great hurricane and its disastrous results to a considerable portion of the state has come to us and to the country. This disaster, however, in no way whatever lessens our conviction as to the great future of Florida and its rapid progress and abounding prosperity in the years ahead.

Every disaster which has come to any American city has resulted in a larger development through increased energy, initiative and the American spirit of determination to conquer difficulties.

When Galveston was so nearly wiped out by the terrific hurricane which resulted in the death of many thousands of its people, it soon met the emergency and has become a far greater Galveston.

When Dayton, Ohio, was almost overwhelmed by the disastrous flood which swept over that place, the people arose in their might to meet the emergency, and Dayton is a far greater place than before the flood.

The same thing was true when thousands were made homeless by the fire of Jacksonville and the greatness is largely the outcome of the spirit of initiative and energy which was brought about by the fire which swept over that city.

Baltimore lost over $100,000,000 in the two-day fire of 1904, but Baltimore of today is a far greater and more prosperous city than it was before that disaster, and much of this is due to the spirit of energy and cooperation brought about by that fire.

San Francisco, almost destroyed by the earthquake and the fire which followed, met the emergency and is a greater and richer and far more populous city than it then was.

The disaster which has struck some portions of Florida, serious as it is for individuals, sad as it is to those who have lost loved ones, will on the whole create a greater enthusiasm for the upbuilding of these communities than ever before. There will be born as there was in Baltimore and in other cities, a new spirit of cooperation and initiative, and energy will come to the front to a greater extent than in the past, and Florida will go forward in its mighty march of progress and prosperity.

In extending to our Florida readers our deepest sympathy, we would express the hope that you did not individually suffer in the loss of property or in the death of loved ones, but if either disaster came to you we sincerely trust that if it was a property loss that it will soon be found more than regained, and if it was loss of some loved one that you may find that comfort and consolation which Heaven alone can give to those who see their loved ones pass on before them into what has well been called, "God's other world."

Sincerely yours,
RICHARD H. EDMONDS,
Editor.

———

There came out of the North immediate sympathy and offers to aid. This from a New York newspaperman as published in the *Fort Lauderdale News*:

A MESSAGE OF CONFIDENCE

Mr. Gilbert T. Hodges, editor of the New York Sun, in a message of sympathy to the residents of the City of Fort Lauderdale, expresses his confidence of an immediate recovery and predicts that the indomitable spirit of our citizens will place Florida upon a still higher and firmer foundation. Mr. Hodges' telegram follows:

"Horace C. Stilwell, Publisher Fort Lauderdale News, Fort Lauderdale, Florida. Your telegram received and you and the residents of Fort Lauderdale have my deepest sympathy. There is a big relief campaign now being conducted in New York and I am sure you will soon feel its helpful effects. The entire country grieves with you on account of this great calamity that has befallen you and you may depend upon the whole country to come to your rescue. This combined with the indomitable spirit of your own citizens will place Florida upon a still higher and firmer foundation and beyond the ravages of a similar disaster, which, let us hope and pray, will never again happen."

(Signed)   G. T. HODGES.

Our friends who mould sentiment in the North have confidence in our future. It is up to us to show that this confidence is not misplaced.

Mrs. C. H. Sears and Son, of Ft. Lauderdale, at Home.

Coast Guard Base Ship, High and "Dry" at Fort Lauderdale.

Nothing Left But the Refrigerator at Hollywood.

"Snowed in" Near Hollywood Casino.

Isolated Devastation Near the Beach at Hollywood.

Hollywood Hotel Used as Hospital.

Devastation Was Complete in Some Parts of Fort Lauderdale.

Bread Line of Amerian Red Cross at Hollywood.

Upper Left: Hurricane Scene Along New River, Ft. Lauderdale.

Center: Come and Pick Out Your Furniture.

Lower Left: Coast Guard Cutter Beached at Ft. Lauderdale.

Upper Right: What Can Be Done With this Home?

Lower Right: Second Story Auto Display at Ft. Lauderdale.

Upper Left: Ft. Lauderdale Home on the River Bank.

Upper Right: Figure It Out For Yourself.

Center: A Bit of the Ft. Lauderdale Business District.

Lower Left: Sloping Floors Have Come Into Vogue.

Lower Right: Ruins of a Yacht at Ft. Lauderdale.

Upper Left: Ft. Lauderdale Apartments Laid Bare.

Upper Right: This Might Have Been a Ft. Lauderdale Home.

Center: An Open Air Theater at Ft. Lauderdale.

Lower Left: These Buildings Escaped With Broken Glass.

Lower Right: A Ft. Lauderdale Side Street.

THE magnitude of storm damage was not fully realized for several days. On Thursday the Citizens' Executive Committee of Miami issued the following appeal to the American people for aid:

To the American People:

The City of Miami is compelled to issue an appeal to the people of the United States for the relief of Miami and Dade County. Six days ago this City of two hundred thousand people was one of the most prosperous, beautiful and delightful communities in this country. Today, as a result of a disastrous tropical hurricane which devastated our coast last Saturday, it lies prostrate.

We have one hundred dead; nearly a thousand patients in the general and emergency hospitals, hundreds of them grievously injured. While conditions are being rapidly restored by means of most wonderful and efficient cooperation of its citizens along all important lines, the problems confronting them are almost insurmountable. Food and other necessary supplies are coming in in great quantities, and we have been blessed by the arrival of a sufficient number of physicians and nurses and ample medical supplies for the immediate present.

But more than five thousand homes have been either entirely destroyed or made unfit for human habitation. Twenty-five thousand people have been rendered homeless. These are being cared for in thousands of instances, by neighbors, who, themselves are suffering. Miami needs money quickly and in large amounts. It needs it to take care of the poor, sick and injured. It needs it to rehabilitate the homes of thousands who have lost everything in the world and who will die of exposure if assistance does not come promptly and amply.

And so, we send out this appeal, believing that the people of this Nation will respond cheerfully and quickly to this great necessity; and on our part, in return, we can only express our appreciation of the wonderful sympathy and aid which is being shown to our sufferers throughout the whole land, and to venture the hope that we may be able, some day and in some way, to reciprocate to other suffering communities the favor we are now asking.

Contributions should be sent either by wire or fast mail addressed to John B. Reilly, Treasurer of the Relief Funds Committee, Miami, Florida, or to The American National Red Cross which has been designated by President Coolidge to raise necessary

The Florida Hurricane
America's Greatest Storm

CHAPTER SEVEN

relief funds, of which James H. Gilman of Miami is treasurer of the local chapter.

The American Red Cross has been placed in full charge of the rehabilitation of Miami and all funds sent for relief will be spent for relief without deductions for administrative costs.

EXECUTIVE COMMITTEE,
FRANK B. SHUTTS, *Chairman,*
E. C. ROMFH, *Mayor,*
RUTH BRYAN OWEN,
F. M. HUDSON,
Formerly President Florida Senate.
JOHN W. WATSON,
Present Senator.
E. B. DOUGLAS, *Chairman Miami Chapter Red Cross,*
R. A. REEDER, *Chairman General Relief Committee.*

THURSDAY, SEPTEMBER 23:

MIAMI is at work today. The Magic City, having recovered its bearing after the shock of the hurricane, has begun to put its house in order. Two hundred thousand people all working at once can accomplish wonders. Everybody is doing something. There are no idle men, and when one is found he is conscripted to the work of clearing away debris or replanting trees. Sheriff Chase posted an order all over the city, stating that "Every Ablebodied Man, Black or White, Must Work."

The emergency hospitals are emptying as injured persons are being discharged when able to go about their duties. Every day now marks the passing of two or three whose injuries proved fatal. But the awful blow has been taken and Miami, broken and groggy, has risen again ready to meet the tasks which confront her.

The official bulletin today, issued by the Citizens' Committee from the Dade County courthouse says:

"The nation is responding generously to the appeal issued by the Executive Committee. Our citizens have responded nobly to their duty and we are certain that no one will abate his efforts until all traces of the disaster are eliminated.

"Roofing still is the most needed building material. Calls have been made upon all near points of shipment and the building supplies committee expects to have on hand 20,000 rolls in the next day or so. There is a sufficient supply of general building material and more has been ordered.

"Miami bakers now are ready to supply all requirements of bread.

"There are 675 tons of ice available today. Probably the same amount will be available tomorrow. It is believed that all ice plants will be in operation within a few days. Meantime, ice is being shipped in.

"About 40,000 gallons of milk are on hand, most of which has been shipped in. Orders for fresh milk for children are being filled at 13 E. Flagler Street. There is a shortage of milk cans, all of which should be returned to supply points as soon as possible.

"We have a large shipment of fresh vegetables and fruits. These should be consumed immediately to avoid waste. All sections in the storm area are invited to make known their needs to the Miami food committee.

"Gasoline restrictions have been lifted. Emergency kerosene stations have been established on Biscayne Drive at the entrance of the P. & O. docks for those in need of the commodity who have automobiles. This will allow those without motor cars to draw upon stations in their neighborhood.

"Our water supply is returning to normal. The supply from the municipal wells at Hialeah was turned on Thursday night and water from this source will be available at Miami Beach Friday. Wells in overflowed localities have been condemned. Water used from such sources must be boiled.

"It is a measure of precaution to boil all water from whatever source. The recommendation that all citizens obtain anti-typhoid vaccination cannot be stressed too urgently. Symptoms of this disease usually would not be felt for about 10 days to two weeks after the storm, and every precaution should be taken meantime.

"We are fully equipped with hospital and medical supplies and have an ample supply of physicians and nurses. It is recommended that all persons apply to their physicians, the relief stations or the hospitals as soon as illness is felt, in order to check contagious disease.

"The health division and sanitary corps of the city, together with the naval militia and coast guard, are clearing the bay of decayed matter. Municipal forces rapidly are clearing the streets of debris. Home owners should pile all debris at an accessible point for collection by the city wagons. Dr A. W. Ziebold, health officer, has returned to the city and is in charge of his division.

"The general relief committee is supplying the needs of about 10,000 persons daily, furnishing them with food, clothing and shelter. A large number of tents have been erected for the homeless. All applicants are being quickly supplied from headquarters at E. Flagler Street and First Avenue.

"The legal aid committee now is comprised of the entire Dade county bar. A number of attorneys always are in attendance. Profiteering and other legal matters pertaining to the emergency should be submitted to this committee. This committee will cooperate with a committee of insurance men to take care of storm insurance adjustments for the small householders. There is no need to pay fees for adjustment of such insurance.

"The general committee is receiving thousands of messages from all parts of the country relative to Miami residents. It is recommended that all residents having relatives out of the city communicate with them at once.

"An employment bureau has been organized at the Elks' club under the direction of R. B. Burdine. An opportunity for work will be given to all who apply. There is no occasion for able-bodied persons going without employment.

"The mails and telegraphic services have been congested, but the former now is able to handle everything with the usual promptness.

"Deplorable exaggerations have emanated from unreliable sources relative to the disaster and some reports have been published all over the country. There is a central bureau of publicity at headquarters from which all authentic statements shall issue, and if you believe there is something that should be reported concerning the storm, bring it here and have its veracity checked. The truth tells a sufficiently shocking story."

Miami's official dead is now placed at 114, but the list of missing has soared to 241. There is no doubt between 50 and 100 of those are gone and will never be found alive. Storm damage in the Greater Miami District is now estimated to be between $80,000,000 and $100,000,000 without taking into account losses to houses and furnishings. These will probably go above $10,-000,000. The loss in all of South Florida will exceed $250,000,000.

More people asked for aid at the Citizens' Relief Headquarters today than on any previous day. Apparently many, dazed at first by the destruction about them, did not realize their condition, while others, restrained for a time by pride, did not at first ask for help. The average call for aid has been less than $100.00. The number of appeals for help is expected to pass the 1,500 mark by Monday.

Several labor unions have offered the services of their members free to those in destitute circumstances.

Donations to the storm relief fund, which is entirely exclusive of Red Cross aid, has totaled $208,391.00. Red Cross funds are pouring in from all sections of the United States and Canada. Benefit performances in theatres are being given from ocean to ocean.

It is estimated about $500,000 damage was sustained by school buildings alone in Dade County. They will open Monday wherever a building is left standing in condition to accommodate pupils.

The downtown business section of Miami shows results of labor on its wounds today. In the outlying districts the work of clearing away tons upon tons of debris is proceeding apace. Thousands of negroes are engaged by the city in the work of clearing streets, straightening up trees and handling refuse.

What Happened to a Hialeah Business House.

The public utilities are not yet working more than 20 per cent, except water, which is running in the mains throughout the entire city. The Florida Power & Light Company, whose losses have summed up $1,200,000, has managed to light the business district and some of the through streets leading north and south. It will be several weeks before the entire city is lighted and given cooking power.

The bankers, who for a few days after the hurricane placed a limit on the amount individuals could withdraw, have thrown business wide open and are even increasing loans to meritorious applicants who wish to rebuild their homes.

Advertisements are appearing in the newspapers by families who wish to adopt orphans whose parents were lost in the hurricane. The dead in Miami have totaled 114, but I have not yet seen a funeral. No doubt they are burying bodies quietly so as not to disturb the morale of the people, and sending them to former homes in the North.

The dead in the entire hurricane belt can now be numbered as follows:

Greater Miami, 114; Homestead, 3; Fort Lauderdale, 26; Moore Haven, 200; Hollywood, 56. Total, 399.

THE DEAD

AT PHILBRICK'S

Alton Bush Little, reporter, Miami Beach Beacon.
Mrs. J. W. McGinnis, Sigmund boulevard, near Coral Gables.
Hattie E. Winslow, 67, of 1847 N. W. 22nd street.
John Petty, 18, of Coral Terrace, west of Coral Gables.
Mrs. Josephine Cocraft, 52, Coral Gables.

Unidentified man found with life preserver around waist on a barge at Collins avenue and 14th street, Miami Beach.
Two women, two boys, one man, unidentified.

AT W. H. COMBS COMPANY.

Lydia Brookshire, 5822 N. W. Eleventh avenue.
Unidentified man, height five feet 11 inches, weight 175 pounds. Had dark hair. Found at Miami Beach.
Frank H. Schwarz of 1028 S. W. 27th court.
Frank Hoskins.
Unidentified woman found dead at Miami Beach. Weight 175, age 50; wore a brown dotted dress trimmed in green.
Benjamin T. Watts, Hialeah.

AT KING UNDERTAKING COMPANY.

Fred Shutts, 35, 1738 S. W. Eighth street.
George Maleet, 34, Hialeah.
Venetian Carter, 1-year-old, of Hialeah.
J. J. Eagan, N. W. 5th street and 3rd avenue.
J. T. Philips, N. W. 21st avenue and 65th street.
Unidentified girl, 3 years old, of Hialeah.
Mrs. Gluck of Homestead.
Three unidentified women of Hialeah.
Two unidentified men of Hialeah.
Two unidentified persons of Miami Beach.

AT GAUTIER'S FUNERAL HOME.

Unidentified woman.
Unidentified man.
Seven unidentified negroes.

AT NORTHSIDE FUNERAL HOME.

Mrs. Tolula A. Roberts, 59th street and N. E. 2nd avenue.
Mrs. Ella Harrison, 42, white Belt Dairy.
Mrs. Edith Baker, N. W. 75th street and 20th avenue.
Mrs. Victoria Roberts, 59th street and N. E. 2nd avenue.
Little Doc Fisher, 39, 1109 N. W. 21st street.
William W. Estey, 60, Miami Shores.
Miss Anny Ballou of Dayton, Ohio.
Mr. Snow, Biscayne Park Estates.
Mr. Whilehurst, Seaboard Park.
A. J. Winnenberg, Biscayne Park, formerly of Burlington, Iowa.
A. J. Harrison, White Belt Dairy.
A. D. Harrison, White Belt Dairy.
Coralyn Ruth Beem, child, 410 N. E. 91st street.
Mrs. Mary A. Hopper, 67, of 7336 N. Miami court.
Four adults have not been identified.
Four children also are unidentified. Two of them were six years old and two younger. Two lived in Miami Shores, one in the Tropics neighborhood and one at Lemon City.

HOLLYWOOD.

H. G. Luther.	Vick Driver.
Mrs. Sarah Head.	L. P. Pool.
G. A. Rogers.	Mrs. L. P. Pool.
Gordon Brown.	Lorena Helem.
Murlean Brown.	Leon Helem.
Mrs. Rhoda Louise Priest.	

DANIA.

Annie Carley.	Peter McAllister.
Mrs. Yeager.	Netty Kielman.
Mrs. R. W. Moore.	Mrs. J. H. Craft.
Moore infant.	Jenny Ferral.
Andrew Hevelock.	Peter Vighes.
Mrs. Cohy.	

HALLANDALE.

Mrs. H. J. Kimball.	Kimball infant.

FORT LAUDERDALE.

W. A. Tellmer.	Mrs. R. D. Crowley.
Mrs. W. A. Tellmer.	J. B. Story.
Robert Tellmer.	Ivan Austin, infant.
Martha Tellmer.	P. E. Gamble.
R. D. Crowley.	Ralph McClure.

THE INJURED.

AT THE McALLISTER HOTEL.

Gwendely Coffe, Miami, laceration of the foot.
Byron Platt, Miami Shores, laceration of the face and body bruises.
Floyd Hazelbater, Hialeah, laceration of the head.
Mrs. Manning, laceration of the face.
Mrs. Jordon, laceration of the right hand.
Fred Gould, paralyzed legs.
Mrs. Louis Marcotte, Hialeah.
H. G. Booske, nail in foot.
Earl Hudson, crushed ribs.
Mrs. Don Lawrence, spine injured.
Isador Lutski, injured on the head.
Alvin McNally, glass in the right foot.
J. D. Hedonsville, hand cut.
Fred Delaney, Hialeah, paralyzed.
William Tomme, bruised right leg.
Mrs. Marie Conner, Hialeah, crushed leg.
S. Meltzer, shoulder injured by fall.
Robert Campbell, body bruises.
Robert Pepper, right foot crushed.
C. N. Henry, body bruises.
Louis Ronch, laceration of the face and two crushed ribs.
Miss Thelma Harris, right side injured.
Max Sikeh, fractured right leg.
J. W. Russell, laceration of the scalp.

Elizabeth Stuart, run down by an automobile, extent of
  injuries unknown.
Fred H. Grove, injured on the head.
A. D. Armond, scraped left leg.
Mrs. T. C. Harless, injured spine.
Mrs. W. L. Sellers, body bruises.
A. E. Bland, fractured ribs.
T. W. Davis, laceration of the face.
Mrs. T. E. Smith, right leg broken.
Mrs. Minnie Shaw, left leg and arm injured.
J. B. Lingefeld, laceration of the head.
W. G. Moore, crushed ribs.
Mrs. T. W. Davis, laceration of the scalp.
Beryl Stegell, fracture of the right leg.
C. H. Bryant, cut finger on the right hand.
L. J. Delaney, finger on the hand cut.
Floyd Delaney, same.
H. M. Dick, Patricia hotel, Miami, right foot injured.
Thomas A. Montgomery, Henrietta towers, laceration
  of the right leg.
John Engstron, 17 S. E. Sixth street, scalp wounds.
Mrs. Martha Kruse, lacerations of the right foot.
J. C. Pickthorn, Hialeah, fracture of the right leg and
  lacerations of the head.
D. Carter, Hialeah, bruised hands and ribs.
Nathan Lewis, 1709 N. W. 2nd street, lacerations of
  the left leg.

Among the injured who have recently been
removed to the hotel are:

G. N. Stein,	Miss Margaret Conner,
Mrs. Evelyn Larsen,	G. W. Davis,
B. Leary,	G. A. Dolan and three
Porter Longston,	children,
S. Mettzer,	Mr. Albert Everle,
W. G. Moore.	Mrs. Albert Everle,
Mrs. J. R. Pattee,	A. R. Fisher,
Louis Ronch,	R. H. Greene,
Mrs. Charles Almquist,	C. K. Glellander,
Rob. G. Campbell,	Mrs. T. C. Harlese,
H. W. Crisp,	Earl Hudson.
S. M. Carpenter,	

HOLLYWOOD.

Mrs. Clyde Blow,	Mrs. Leo O'Day,
J. O. Black,	O'Day infant,
Jessie Carnegie,	T. D. Ellis, Jr.,
Mrs. J. E. Colwell,	Walter Glenn,
Colwell infant,	Frederick Hudson,
Mrs. W. F. Duncan,	Maxwell Hall,
Duncan infant,	R. W. Moore.
Leo O'Day,	

It is expected more than 100 bodies will be
recovered in all of South Florida when wreckage is removed and yachts are brought to the
surface. The entire death list will not exceed
500.

The Rotary Club of Tokyo, Japan, today extended its sympathies to Miami. A message was
received from King George, of England.

The military have been withdrawn from the
Miami area, and 75 soldiers who served this city
well entrained today for points in North Florida.

Work of clearing the harbor for ocean-going
shipping is being rushed. It is estimated 200
boats and 75 houseboats went down in Biscayne
Bay during the storm.

Carl G. Fisher today made the announcement
he will spend $2,000,000 for the rehabilitation
of Miami Beach. Mr. Fisher invested his entire
fortune of a similar amount fourteen years ago
in establishing Miami Beach and making of it
America's most famous resort city. Managers
of all the Fisher hotels are here to take charge
of these hotels, which is two months earlier than
they came down any other year.

None of the large Miami hotels have suffered
seriously from the storm. An air of optimism prevails among the managers. They are unanimous
in the prediction that the coming season will be
Miami's greatest and they are united in the
effort to provide better accommodations at a lower rate than ever before.

Newspapers of the city are eloquent in editorial praise of the linemen of the Florida Power
& Light Company who are working night and
day to restore utilities to the citizens. The heroes
of this disaster can never be counted, and linemen will be near to or head the list.

Miami's list of missing persons has grown to
241 and is as follows:

Adams, B. L.	Elliott boy, about 12
Adams, F. W.	Elliott girl, about 7
Allen, David B.	Elliott, Elizabeth
Armstrong, William	Eurman, Capt. Fred
Bailey, C. L.	Eurman, J. O.
Barnett, E. M.	Ewine, Henry
Bauermann, J.	Farrar, Mrs. Jule
Bandrimer, J.	Fisher, Carter
Best, Stanley	Fleming, Richard
Benway, Mr. and Mrs.	Floyd, Aaron B.
Herbert	Forrest, Mr. and Mrs.
Beuchler, E. C.	Edwin
Biggs, Stonewall	Fostler, Paul, wife, Marge
Boatwright, Raymond	Gailey, Ted
Bogan, Dr. and Mrs. Clif-	Gano, Mr. and Mrs. Walter
ford	and child
Brown, Robert	Garrison, Mrs. Lillian
Brownie, E. W.	Gohman, Beatrice
Bright, Adrion	Goldberg, Herman, wife
Brushell, Mrs. J. G.	and two children
Bryson, Daniel J.	Grace, Miss Vila
Brodtkurb, Frede	Grampp, Elsa K.
Buckman, Kate	Grant, Robert
Buckman, Lila	Gray, E. S.
Burks, R. L.	Hale, Mrs. Ben
Blaley, James	Hale, Mrs. Ester
Carlstone, E. C.	Hall, H.
Carruther, Mr. and Mrs.	Hamilton, Mr. and Mrs.
Christian, Bruce	R. W. and five children
Clark, Albert and Mary	Harrison, Mrs. J. E.
Clark, Otis B.	Hazen, Thelma
Charland, A.	Hill, W. A.
Coe, Otto G.	Hodgson, Jack and wife,
Cornell, William E.	Geraldine
Cox, R. H.	Hoffinon, Mr. and Mrs. and
Crouch, Mrs. Ivan	sister
Crouse, Edwin L.	Holden, Russell
Cunningham, Charles	Holmes, Enoch T.
Curry, John	Hood, Herbert, or H. I.
Dabaut, Mrs. E.	Hudgins, Joe, and two
Davis, Frank Patterson,	children
Delay, T. W.	Johansen, Axel
Dixon, Mrs. Margaret	Johansen, J.
Dority, R. H., wife and	Johanansen, S.
child	Johnson, Douglas
Doughtry, M. M.	Johnson, Dr. L. C.
Doughtry, Mr. and Mrs.	Johnson, Mrs. Rabun,
S. L. and three boys.	Jones, A. and family
Ehlinder, Mr. and Mrs.	Kopke, Walter
Oscar	Lacey, W. G.

Lafkowitz, A.
Lanigan, John T.
Lane, Mr. and Mrs. F. E.
Lee, Wallace and wife, Dolores
Lee, Robert E.
Lewis, Emily
Lilly, W. K.
Lord, Elmore
Lunts, Charles
Lazar, Mrs. L. and five children
Lewis, C. T.
Lenoir, Lila
Laxson, Mr. and Mrs. W. C.
McCord, Neal
McMahon, John D.
Majia, J. R. and wife
Maddox, Fred
Madison, Mrs. Eugene
Mitchell, Mrs. Dorothy
Mitchell, Frank
Morris, Phyllis
Munroe, R. D.
Malin, Mrs. Elizabeth
Minor, C. L.
Newell, Alex
Neylon, Mr. and Mrs. John
Oldfield, and two children
Ogan, J. E.
Parker, Noble H. and wife
Patrick, R. C.
Paddock, Howard, and wife
Patterson, Frank
Pritchard, Joseph
Philbin, Mrs. Sara and daughter
Parrow, George
Parker, Mrs. T. A.
Parker, J. W.
Raap, Mrs. A.
Rucker, Tom
Remy, Mrs. Henry
Rife, Joe
Rubinstein, Charles
Ragsdale, Barney
Roobuguez, Remuldo
Robinson, Anna Lee
Robinson, Charles
Rosenberg, Julius
Robinson, Houston L.

Rushin, Frank
Robbins, William W.
Rogers, George A.
Rogers, E. F.
Russell, Miss Elizabeth
Smith, Evelyn
Shepard, Ben and Mary
Shepard, Romeo
Shuster, Fred
Sledd, Dr.
Smith, A. David
Stickler, James and family
Stacey, Russell
Swert, George
Spring, Mrs. Edward
Stephens, George
Shaw, Ezra
Shaw, Elliott
Schwartz, Sam
Stewart, Herschel
Toms, J. P.
Turnage, Derenia
Todd, Katherine A.
Toomey, Helen
Toomey, Gertrude
Toomey, Mr. and Mrs. D. H.
Townes, William
Thompson, Mrs. Cora
Taylor, Ernest L.
Taylor, Sadie Ayres and father
Teague, Archie
Wheeler, Robert, Donald and Herbert
Whidder, Mr. and Mrs. Jack
Whitting, Julia
Welch, Mrs. E. R.
White, Oscar and wife
White, Paul
White, Mallie
Windahl, T.
Walter, L. A. and family
Warren, Gathen
Williams, Ralph J.
Williams, J. F.
Waller, Grady W.
Young, Harold
Young, H. J.
Zobel, Harriett
Zimmerman, W. C. and wife

Officials of Miami, Miami Beach and surrounding towns in the devastated area have distinguished themselves in this emergency. When the terrible hurricane had completed its work of death and destruction there were only the county sheriff's office and city police to maintain a semblance of order and contend with the predatory element which takes advantage of calamity and confusion to get in its criminal work. Hundreds of men presented themselves for duty as special officers. By noon of Sunday there were more ununiformed officers on duty and guns in evidence on the streets than one could count. When it is considered that among those recruits, were nervous and excitable men who had spent a night of horror, guarding the lives of families and friends from the terrors of the gale, their coolness and restraint is to be commended. Only a few sporadic cases of indiscriminate shooting on the part of special officers have been reported. Sheriff Henry Chase, Leslie H. Quigg, chief of the Miami police, and R. H. Woods, chief of the Miami Beach police, were in charge of the situation until martial law was declared with Major Robert N. Ward in command. Military headquarters were established at the county court house. Here passes were issued to those who, aiding in rescue and relief work, had to be on the streets after six o'clock in the evening.

Corps of special officers guarded both ends of the Venetian Causeway Saturday, Sunday and Monday, allowing to pass only those who were carrying water and food, medical supplies, or were armed with a pass. There was some confusion when the military refused to honor the passes previously issued by the police department, but there was reason and consideration on both sides and few arrests resulted.

HEALTH SUGGESTIONS.

(Circulated by the City of Miami Health Division.)

The following suggestions are proposed so that the citizens of Miami may aid in cleaning up the city and preventing the outbreak of any epidemic that may threaten:

Collect Garbage and Refuse.—Place in a receptacle of some kind and put it where trucks can easily pick it up. Trucks are working day and night. If the truck does not come when the householder thinks it should, don't be impatient. It will be done at the earliest possible moment.

Where Small Areas of Water Exist.—The persons living in the vicinity can oil these pools with kerosene or crank case oil. The city mosquito squad can not cover the city soon enough to prevent all mosquito breeding, so it will be necessary for the citizens to help. In apartment houses and hotels where there are basements, these should be pumped out as soon as possible and the floors and walls disinfected to eliminate odors.

Tourist Camp Owners.—Can assist greatly in the work of cleaning up by using their own or hired trucks. This they should do in the interest of their tenants.

In Unsewered Districts.—Where health guard toilets are in use, the city trucks will begin Tuesday night to clean the cans and remove the contents.

Restaurants.—And other food dispensing places can do their part by avoiding serving tainted foods. There is no necessity for serving spoiled food as the food supply is adequate. Restaurants should collect spoiled food and wet packages of such things as biscuits and other cereals and have them ready when the garbage trucks arrive. There have been instances where citizens have not cooperated with our inspectors. This is deplorable and has necessitated harsh measures in a few instances.

Samples of Water.—Are being examined daily from all city wells which are in operation and from residences in each locality served by city wells in order to keep a check on the condition of the mains. Water is being examined also from ten or twelve private wells which are being used by large numbers of people.

(Signed) W. A. CLAXTON, M.D.,
Chief, Division of Health.

Approved: ERNEST COTTON.

White Belt Dairy—South's Finest—in Ruins.

Editorial in the *Miami Tribune* of Friday, September 24th:

REST SUNDAY, WORK MONDAY

Eyes of the entire world are turned in sympathy toward Miami for the first time in the history of this modern city. Editorial comment from newspapers all over the United States show that America feels that America has been dealt a blow, not that Miami alone felt the storm's fury. Many of them have carried wild newspaper stories. Be patient with them. The wires were down, they printed what they could get, and out of what they printed arose in the hearts of the American people a great desire to help Miami. Editorials in newspapers, when they show a singleness of thought throughout a nation, reflect the sentiment of the people, and the newspapers outside of Miami have been kind to this distressed city.

No city would care to profit in a mercenary manner, from disaster. Miami does not wish to do this. But Miami should capitalize upon the sympathy that is being extended her. She will need sympathy and financial assistance in the coming days of reconstruction. Miami's people, true heroes that they were, set about at once to rebuild their city, and the result of their work may be seen in the streets today.

Miamians have been living on sheer nerve, going for hours and days without sleep, and the period of hysteria failed to materialize under the strain. Hysteria is expected in times of stress and its presence here was almost negligible.

But the sheer nerve must give way. The people must have rest. Now is the really critical time for Miami. Let us exercise every care that the rest period does not precede a period of fatal lethargy. Sunday, the day after tomorrow, is our day of rest. Every Miamian should make use of it, rest, worship, and prepare the mind and body for next week's gigantic task of rebuilding where this week's rubbish has been cleared away.

Moore Haven's Main Street After the Storm, Monday, September 20th, 1926.

Havoc of Hurricane on Moore Haven's Only Line of Steel, A. C. L. Railroad.

THE STORY OF MOORE HAVEN.

HAVE you ever been in the Everglades, Florida's great morass, where the canals stretch like ribbons of silver under the moon, and the saw-grass swamps are flat and still in the hush of the tropical night?

If you should leave West Palm Beach today and proceed west along the famous Conner's Highway, you would pass through the edges of the great swamp to the shores of Lake Okeechobee, second largest fresh-water lake in the United States. If, after leaving Canal Point at the junction of the lake with the West Palm Beach Canal, you should skirt the great body of water to its Southwestern shore, you would come to the ruins of what once was a thriving young Florida city.

Moore Haven was a homey little town, smug and prosperous, and its 1,200 inhabitants were bound together in the fraternity of the pioneer. They were honest and simple people used to the daily toil of earning their living, and a little bit more, out of the muck lands that surrounded their little city. They had built a modern town here on the fringe of the great Florida civilization. They had modern conveniences, such as water, electricity, sidewalks, hard-surfaced streets, schools and churches. Moore Haven was looked upon with pride by other sections of the State. Had not its pioneers shown to the world the unbelievable richness of the Everglades!

Had you visited Moore Haven before September 17, 1926, you would have seen the clean black fields from which four crops of truck per year are garnered. You would have met and chatted with men and women from all sections

The Florida Hurricane
America's Greatest Storm

❦

CHAPTER EIGHT

of the United States who had come to this Everglades town to live quietly and comfortably in the great silence of Southwestern Florida. You would have seen away to the East the shimmering waters of Lake Okeechobee, flat, lazy and apparently innocent. The lake that afforded a living through the fishing industry to those of Moore Haven's population who did not till the soil. Little would you then have suspected that before 24 hours had passed, the waters of this great lake, lashed into a mad frenzy by a terrific gale, would sweep over the little city and leave a host of corpses in the muck-mire amid the wreckage of their former homes.

In every great disaster, there is always some spot upon which the spectre of Death seems to take his position, and from which he directs the work of destruction all around. In the Florida hurricane, this spot was Moore Haven. It seems that the storm gods who shrieked through Florida's frightful night chose this little Everglades town to demonstrate in memorable completeness their awful and merciless might.

On the fateful night of September 17, a pale moon cast a weird glow over the great expanse of the Everglades of South Florida. The people of Moore Haven went to their two movie theatres or remained in the quiet seclusion of their homes. Young couples strolled along the dykes, their amorous eyes flashing out over the gentle rippling waters of the lake.

Moore Haven's citizens went to bed between

10 o'clock and midnight. Already a report had come from Miami and West Palm Beach that a hurricane was approaching, but they did not worry. A hurricane was not to be greatly feared. Had not their engineers told them the dykes were of sufficient height and strength to withstand the severest storm?

By one o'clock on the morning of Saturday, September 18, the wind had risen to an alarming velocity. Lake Okeechobee was licking the top of the dykes. The gale was rising every minute. Criers with flashlights went through the streets shouting a warning to residents to rise and stand by, ready for anything. A half-hour later the wires went down, and Moore Haven was isolated from the world. Just before communication was cut off a message had come that Miami had been wiped out, and the terrific gale was moving westward. People of Moore Haven then began to realize that the crest of the storm had not yet reached them. They also knew their town and the menacing lake might be directly in the path of the most devastating storm in Florida's history.

Upwards rose the wind. Higher and higher the great, plunging waves of the lake were dashed against the dykes—against them, over them, through them — the dykes had broken. With the wind at more than 100 miles per hour, the mad waters rushed over the too-low protection, through the great gaps and breaks of the broken dykes, and swept over Moore Haven and its helpless populace to a depth of fifteen feet. Scores of men, women and children were drowned like rats in a trap in the first rush of the flooding waters, which came like a wall through and over the dykes. Those caught in their beds

Wind and Water Made Devastation Complete at Mocre Haven.

Main Street of Moore Haven on September 20th.

had not a chance for life as the crazed elements drove the very lake through their windows and doors. The raging flood whipped into a foamy frenzy surged through the streets.

To the roofs! That was the only place of refuge in Moore Haven; and that is where the frightened, hysterical, terror-crazed people tried to go. It was dark—dark as pitch—black as ink. Fathers and mothers trying to get to the roofs of their homes, or seizing floating wreckage, whipped and buffeted by wind and water, weak and terror-stricken, saw their children torn from their arms and swirled away in the raging torrent. Many gave up the fight to stay on the roofs in the face of the tempest and, releasing their hold on shingles and tiles, slipped with a moan into the roaring waters. Some fainted with fear and toppled into the flood. Many thought the end of the world had come and gave up. The human brain cannot picture, nor words describe, the plight of those hundreds of helpless people in the fastness of the Everglades during the five hours of terror on September 18, 1926. In other sections of the storm's path, those who lived back from the ocean had only the wind to combat, but Moore Haven battled five frightful hours with wind, water and darkness. And no human being who did not pass through it can imagine or ever know what that night was like. No abatement; no slowing down for a second. Five continuous hours of rushing, roaring, slashing, deadly wind that drove fear and terror into the strongest hearts. Slowly came daylight over the ghastly scene of death and devastation. More than one hundred and fifty corpses lay in the mire. Scores of them had been swept far out in the reaches of the Everglades. Thousands of

vultures swarmed overhead ready to devour the bodies of Moore Haven's dead citizenry. No food — no drinking water — no clothing — no medical supplies. Survivors of the night looked with puzzled, expressionless eyes over their desolated homes and the bodies of their dead. The strongest set about with jaded bodies to minister what first aid was available to the suffering women and children survivors.

The first relief train from Sebring, slowly made its way toward Moore Haven Saturday evening, several hours after the hurricane had abated. A haggard, hysterical populace met it and many flung themselves in the abandon of fatigue on the floors of the coaches. Bodies that could be found and identified were taken to Avon Park for burial.

Many corpses were taken from the muck-mire mutilated and partly eaten by vultures. Sanitary conditions became the worst possible. Crazed men

refused to leave the town until they had found the bodies of loved ones. Many had to be forced onto the train by soldiers of the National Guard who took charge of the situation.

It was days before the waters receded at Moore Haven. Although the dykes provided some protection from incoming flood waters the canals afforded no outlet by which the water could return to the body of the lake. Governor John W. Martin visited the stricken area and, on inspection, ordered the military to remain in control for an indefinite period, and the entire populace was ordered from Moore Haven and all of Glades County, until sanitary conditions could be partly restored.

The work of recovering bodies was perhaps the most gruesome ever experienced by rescue parties anywhere in this country. Vultures, buzzards and snakes of the Everglades had taken their toll of decomposing human flesh. Corpses were found in parts miles from their homes, prone in the saw-grass swamps or half buried in the soggy muck. Others were retrieved from the canals as they came to the surface days after the storm, but identification was often impossible, because of the toll that had been taken by the earth, water and elements.

Twenty miles west of Moore Haven on a point of high pine land overlooking the Florida Everglades there is a new cemetery today. In this spot under the pine trees, there are rows of homely graves that bear no names, the final resting places of Moore Haven's unidentified dead. Will the spirits of these ride the zephyrs of the night in Florida's future, and look down on a new Everglades where floods will not sweep over human beings?

One of Moore Haven's Few Standing Homes.

Military Headquarters at Moore Haven Were Established at This Unwrecked House.

Relief Workers Entering Moore Haven, Monday, September 20th, 1926.

Removing Bodies From Watery Graves in Moore Haven.

Preparing Last Resting Place for Moore Haven's Unidentified Dead.

Soldiers Removing Another of Moore Haven's Dead From the Canal.

The Unidentified Dead Were Laid in Rows, in the Pinelands 20 Miles West of Moore Haven, by Their Neighbors.

Governor John W. Martin (in white shirt) Entering Moore Haven on Inspection Trip After Disaster.

And so . . . . South Florida faces the future. Her citizens have girded their loins (some of them in queer garb to be sure) for the herculean task of raising from the ruins of their once charming country, new homes in which to enjoy Florida's incomparable climate, new cities, larger, greater and safer than the old.

There is much sadness in South Florida— much lamentation for the passing of loved ones and the death of hopes. But there is no pessimism, no rush to leave this beauteous land. The general feeling is that Miami and South Florida were entitled in the natural order of things to one catastrophe, and now that is past.

It is perhaps trite to say that a disaster such as this can benefit a community. But, yet, there is in the souls of men a quiet determination to conquer the forces of nature, as far as is possible to human beings. That determination springs into action immediately a catastrophe rouses it from lethargy.

Miami and South Florida have had their share of success and bow before the inevitable workings of the Law of Compensation. They have paid their price, and the future now lies golden before them.

Tears for the dead, relief for the suffering and unwavering faith in the future are the watchword of the hour. People from all over America and Canada have rushed to the aid of Florida in her hour of travail just as they streamed down the highways into her soft, tropical sunshine during the years of her great, growing activity. South Florida is not merely a locality. It is a national institution. There was not a city, town or hamlet in this Nation that did not contain worried souls when the first news was

The Florida Hurricane
America's Greatest Storm

CHAPTER NINE

flashed out that a great disaster had visited here. The population of this section is representative of every state in the Union, every province of Canada, and all countries of Europe. Hundreds of thousands have come here to enjoy the world's finest climate and it will take more than several such hurricanes to deter them from remaining.

The hurricane with its disastrous ravages did this one great benefit—it has knitted Florida into a closer Union with its sister states, some of which during the years of its growth dealt with it a little unkindly, though according to the deepest inclinations of human nature. One touch of nature—or human suffering—makes the whole world kin. We have proved that we can stand up under punishment here in Florida, and we have found that when we are temporarily down our fellow-citizens in other states will help us to our feet and back into the fight.

All of South Florida is grateful, deeply and thoroughly grateful for the aid rendered us in our hour of trouble. There is one way we can repay—by utilizing this aid together with our own brain and muscle in rebuilding our beautiful cities into still finer havens of comfort and enjoyment so that those who have helped us will reap the benefits of their generosity in years to come.

The spirit of Florida is breathed out from the pages of its newspapers these terrible days. I will include here editorials from Miami, Palm Beach, and other Florida newspapers published since last Saturday, the day of the hurricane.

The morale of Miami's citizens was bolstered up by the following editorials in the *Miami Daily News* of Monday, September 27th:

THE POWER OF HOPE

The greatest asset possessed by the people of this country is hopefulness. When the earth trembled beneath their feet and buildings tottered and fell about them, the people of San Francisco hopefully prayed for the sunlight, that they might bind up the wounds of their injured, bury their dead and start life anew.

When a hurricane swept the waters of a gulf over the homes of happy and contented Galveston and, receding, left a trail of corpses strewn for miles along the beach, Galveston citizens tenderly and tearfully consigned to mother earth the 5,000 who had perished and assembled in a great mass meeting to discuss means for preventing a repetition of the tragedy. They were hopeful that some means might be found whereby the lives and property of those remaining would be protected. That hopefulness brought forth a giant seawall which today shields the city of Galveston from ravages of the ever-restless gulf.

When a flood descended upon the city of Dayton, and human lives and homes were lost beneath its maddening rush; when lights went out and stalwart men tore from their backs their own clothing to protect the cold and shivering forms of women and little children crouched about them; when suffering and death and destruction seemed everywhere, one man emerged with the signal needed to still their fears—the banner of Hope. Homes were twisted upon foundations, their interiors deep in mud and slime deposited by the waters as a sickening reminder of their power to destroy. Here a man set about hopefully clearing the street in front of his home. Inside, the wife dragged forth to the sunshine all that remained of household goods— and she sang a song of hope. An hour later a score were so engaged. Before the day had ended, the whole city was struggling hopefully back into the path of happiness and contentment.

Eight days ago, when there came out of the seas a storm more severe than the southland has yet experienced, and when the roofs above Miami residents were swept away; when tidewater drove everything before it and mingled human life among its debris, one man, John Burke, viewed the destruction of the home in which he had found his greatest happiness. Beside him on a lawn piled high with torn and twisted foliage stood his dearest possessions, his wife and children. He looked at the wreck of a lifetime of saving and sacrifice. All that remained of it was a bit of jagged wall, no higher than his head. This was still smooth with the stucco which had served as its covering. Going to the tumbled heap which a few hours before had served as a garage, he burrowed into the ruins and came forth with a can of paint. From a twisted and ruined palm tree he plucked a frond. And with this as a brush, he painted on the bit of bare wall of his wrecked home a message of hopefulness to those heavy of heart who stood in the street in wonderment:

"Wiped Out, But Still Smiling!"

That was the message of hope John Burke, railroader, Miamian, American, painted on the wreck of a once happy home. That is the message those in the street paused to read and in reading found an inspiration. Within a few hours, almost as quickly as the great storm had swept the city, John Burke's message of hopefulness swept it, but with a happier hand. And Miami smiled through her tears, just as San Francisco and Galveston and Dayton smiled amid their sorrows, and with the same spirit of hopefulness they displayed in building anew, Miami is carrying on.

Up from the ruins of the nation's wrecked playground will come a more beautiful and a more substantial city. Nature will heal the wounds the winds have wrought, for ours is a tropic land, and ferns and palms and flowers have all the year in which to grow. Buildings hurriedly constructed and without thought of the future have perished, along with those long since made frail through years of service. Homes and business structures of a substantial type quickly will replace these. New methods will be used in both building and beautification of our city by the sea. Though it has been at an awful cost, Miami in many ways will profit through her sad experience.

Hopefulness, individually or collectively, is the greatest of all assets. It is the greatest earthly asset, because it is the foundation of earthly happiness. There can be no happiness where there is no hope. It is the greatest spiritual asset, because it points to eternal happiness.

"Wiped Out, But Still Smiling!"

The slogan of hopefulness through which will come a greater Miami. The slogan through which every heart can find happiness when fate reveals the roughness of her hand.

MIAMI'S REAL SPIRIT.

The spirituality and the devout faith in an All-Wise Providence of the stricken people of Greater Miami never were demonstrated more feelingly and more wonderfully than they were Sunday.

Work, work, and yet more work, was to be, and was being, done; but the Christian citizenry of this great city and of the surrounding territory seized the opportunity to attend religious services in all churches left standing in the wake of the hurricane and in community assemblages held in the open, under the beneficent sunshine of Heaven.

Surrounded by mute evidence of devastation and death, and not unmindful of the physical suffering and mental sorrow that had come upon them, these bodies of strong and determined people re-expressed their faith in Almighty God and besought Him to give them additional strength to bear the burdens thrust upon them.

The meetings Sunday constituted a wonderful spiritual awakening. They meant that added energy, force and determination would be put into the work of rehabilitation, that widespread losses soon would be restored and that the fine municipalities, so seriously damaged, would rise again in finer and more substantial form than at any time in their history.

It was recalled at every one of the Sunday assemblages that many American cities in the past had suffered from catastrophic disasters, and that in every instance they not only survived and recovered from their difficulties and suffering, but had risen to heights of success, prosperity and magnificence never before attained.

Chicago, Galveston, San Francisco and Baltimore, all devastated by conflagration, earthquake or tidal flood, were instanced as examples of the marvelous recovery from terrible calamities. Those outstanding examples of indomitable courage and unconquerable spirit will be stressed again by the citizens of the Miami district.

Lon W. Crow, president of the Chamber of Commerce, felicitously expressed this idea when he declared:

"Community faith and pride remain solid as the rock on which the city stands. Our eyes are to the future and they see only the beauty and enduring qualities of an enlarged and more substantial Miami. 'Bigger and Better' will be the slogan of our new building program."

Miami has risen whole-heartedly and with magnificent spirit to the greatest emergency it ever confronted.

Already it has achieved wonders in its work of rehabilitation. That work is going forward 24 hours of every day, and, with the spiritual as well as the physical efforts of our people thoroughly aroused, as they now are, the suffering and terror of the catastrophe of a few days ago will become in a brief time only a memory.

Governor James M. Cox, of Ohio, sent the following editorial Friday to his Miami newspaper, the *Daily News*:

STORM AND SUNSHINE.
BY GOV. JAMES M. COX
(In Dayton Daily News)

The only hope, apparently, which the country can entertain is that the Florida storm was less severe in its consequences to human life and property than first reports indicate. When the elements sever communication with any territory having a considerable population, the picture of disaster is sometimes overdrawn. It's a case of imagination being worked up to the point of what might be possible. Another thing not to be counted clearly out of consideration is that the first view of a water or wind visitation carries one's idea of the loss much beyond the real toll which nature has taken.

The first reports from Dayton during the flood of 1913 were that the city, for all practical purposes, was destroyed. Desolation seemed complete. Streets from curb to curb were covered with debris. The loss to stocks of merchandise and to buildings ran over $100,-000,000. Fire had left its black path. Those who had lived through the days of despair were numbed in their sensibilities.

Man, however, is a wonderful animal. In the case of Dayton, where from the outside it seemed that human life stood no chance, and that the loss would be at least 10,000 souls, the mass of humanity, with ingenuity and courage inborn, preserved itself and the death list was only a little more than 100. It was springtime and the people quickly went to work. Wreckage disappeared as if by magic. The homing instinct asserted itself. The individuals took care of their own habitat, and the organized agencies of society of the public thoroughfares.

The Ohio flood, as a matter of fact, was much worse than a fire, because there was no insurance against loss from water. If the very center of Dayton had been burned to the ground, there would have been a greater toll of life, but there would have been less impairment of private and corporate wealth. The year 1913, with the merchants and with the community generally in Dayton, was the most prosperous ever experienced up until that time.

At the outset, the skeptic insisted that Dayton and the Miami valley particularly would be advertised to the world as a dangerous place to live, notwithstanding there had not been a flood scarcely worth the name in almost 50 years.

The sort of cities which grew out of this calamity is

but another indication of the unconquerable spirit of the race. The city of San Francisco was well nigh leveled by earthquake. Fire completed the work of destruction. There were predictions that there would be no survival of the city for the reason that the earth's surface was too thin, that earthquakes were too common, and that there was no need of the peril involved. Therefore, San Francisco would dwindle to the limits of a small place. The answer to this apprehension was the harbor. The western people smiled through their tears and with high purpose addressed themselves to the work of rehabilitation. The result is too well known to need any reference to it.

And so it will be with Miami and Florida. This great health-giving empire, blessed with its sunshine and fertility, as well as bedeviled with its tropical storms, as the north is with its cyclones, will display that resiliency of spirit and courage which is typical of our modern settlements. Florida is beloved by those who live there and have been there. It is in close contact with the West Indies and with South America. Miami is just off the great Atlantic traffic lane. A good harbor is being transformed into an excellent one, and the inexorable law of trade and commerce has decreed for it a great future. A city, like an individual, never appreciates inherent strength until the test comes. Wreckage quickly disappears in the face of human industry and courageous purpose.

Where many people were disposed to treat Miami and south Florida particularly with ridicule because of the collapse of an unnatural real estate boom, they will turn now in sympathy to the permanent population. This will be followed in brief time with an admiration, nation-wide, of the indomitable pluck which will not only bring restoration but prepare the way for a development which was not even apparent before the disaster fell.

The heroism of Miami, bowed down by disaster, is breathed in this editorial in the *Jacksonville Journal* of Thursday:

HEROIC MIAMI.

Miami, stricken by severe hurricane, with a toll of dead, piles of debris, quickly sent the word that she could take care of her own problems. The spirit was commendable, but that city should not be allowed to drain its resources to carry the load beyond the duty of other portions of the state, that were untouched, to help. The courage that Miami has shown to repair her losses and to go forward in the face of disaster should be an inspiration to the rest of Florida to forge onward. The thought of Miami is to rebuild. The rest of the state will applaud her efforts and it is confident that a short time will see the same old Miami of old, entertaining thousands of visitors who will go there for the winter to bask in the sunshine. Heavy as the blows of gales may be, it is surprising how quick recovery can be made. Miami will show the rest of the country how speedily it can be done. Of that all Florida is confident. Miami has proved her heroism.

These editorials in the *Miami Daily News* of Friday following the storm breathe the indomitable spirit of the Magic City:

THE CITY'S SPIRIT

Miami's place in the firmament of municipalities is fixed. The city has passed through the fire of disaster and its metal has come unscathed from the test. The spirit of the people of Miami is unconquerable.

Newspaper reports have listed few instances of profiteering and petty pilfering that have followed the storm. They have been very few. Large space has been given to the rush of aid through the Citizens' Relief committee and the national Red Cross, which has done so much to lighten the load of an overburdened people.

But the song of self-sacrifice, of neighborly kindness, of individual self-effacement in the face of an abnormal condition has remained unsung.

If "one touch of nature makes the whole world kin," then Saturday's hurricane has welded the people here into a kinship so close that the city need never fear the integrity of its population. Race, creed and partisanship have been forgotten in the common need.

Instances multiply to prove the courage which grew from the storm's wreckage.

A grocer whose stock had been all but ruined by the elements scrawled this sign on his boarded window as soon as the winds had abated:

"No increase in prices. If you are destitute, it's free."

In a community of Allapattah, which is largely given over to the homes of workers at building trades, men refused to leave their homes to accept work at good pay until after they had made the homes of their neighbors habitable.

In Coral Gables, the mistress of a residence that had been flooded during the storm was surprised yesterday morning when her neighbor's maid appeared at her door and offered to aid in clearing up the home. Her own work was done, this colored worker said.

Restaurants, which had been doing good business at a fixed charge, began soon after the storm to reduce that price to barely the cost of serving the meals. Many of them displayed signs offering to serve those in need without cost.

It takes more than great buildings and charming vistas to make a city; it takes more than a mass of people to make a community; it takes more than broad avenues and thronged stores to mark the achievement of a civic ideal. That Miami has these additional qualities has been proven.

Hearts as strong as the hearts of Miami never can be beaten.

ALL CREDIT TO THEM

When the hurricane struck Miami a week ago, the mayor of the city was absent.

Before the storm had passed, James H. Gilman, president of the Bank of Bay Biscayne, in his capacity as acting mayor, had mobilized the forces of the city, organized a relief committee and set in motion the wheels of a machine which functioned so smoothly and swiftly that before we knew it Miami was operating on its accustomed schedule.

There is no record in the disaster history of this country of such a swift recovery as is recorded here. The spirit that pervaded this city is without equal.

Standing shoulder to shoulder with Acting Mayor Gilman was H. Leslie Quigg, chief of police, who, with the aid of a highly trained police department, maintained law and order, succored the injured, housed the homeless, fed the hungry and wrote a chapter of efficient and faithful service that will survive in the book of time.

There was no waste of valuable time in Miami when disaster struck, because Gilman was at the helm. There was no panic; there was no tangle of red tape; there was no fear in the hearts of Miamians—because Gilman was at the helm.

There was no orgy of looting; there was no untold disorder on the streets; there was no reign of terror—because Quigg was on the job.

Sheriff Henry Chase and his deputies measured up in the emergency.

Miami today is thankful that such men as Gilman and Quigg were available in its great emergency.

LET THEM KNOW.

The telegraph wires have been burdened with messages from every section of the country making anxious inquiry as to the fate of persons who were residents in the district before the hurricane.

Newspaper offices have been deluged with requests for information of this character.

It is impossible for people in distant places to visualize the difficulties in obtaining information of this character at this time. They do not realize that thousands of addresses have been changed by the storm; and that new addresses are not available.

In spite of these difficulties much progress has been made. Many requests for information have been answered and the minds of friends and relatives relieved.

But this work can be speeded up if the people of Miami who have lost their homes will get in touch with their former homes by wire and let those who are inquiring about them know that they are alive and well.

Newspapers in every city will be glad to act as agents for people in this city who desire to make general announcements of their safety or their losses. Newspapers in Miami will give every assistance that they can.

Readers of the Miami Daily News who have any information about people whose names are found in the "information wanted" items which appear in this newspaper will help if they will report this information direct to inquiries or send the information to the office of the Daily News.

This newspaper is burdened with detail, but it will never be too busy to relieve the fears or settle the doubts of those who are worried because of inability to get in touch with those they love here.

Editorials in the *Miami Herald* of Thursday:

IN TODAY'S NEWS.

Miami appeals to the world for help. But Miami also pushes ahead in the present emergency and aids herself. The true spirit of cooperation prevails, and the mutual welfare of all is superior to the private interests of any individual. The merchants are proving splendid. Profiteering has properly been prohibited. But manufacturers, wholesalers, retailers are going still farther. Instead of prices rising in the face of the increased demand and lessened supply, they are actually lower. Foodstuffs are reasonable, and where there is dire distress they are provided free. Clothing costs drop. The same is true in every line. Miami becomes a gigantic corporation moving and working together for the benefit of everyone.

In the press of the United States there still remains only one news story of supreme importance, and that is the Florida hurricane. All other events have given way to accounts from Miami and nearby stricken communities. The entire nation is vitally interested in conditions here, not only because of the universal sympathy when such tragedies occur, but also due to the personal concern in our welfare. Florida and Miami are national institutions, not local. People are here

from everywhere. There has been anxiety in homes throughout this country, for hardly a city or hamlet in America is unrepresented in the cosmopolitan population. When the storm struck Florida it drove terror into the hearts of the United States. And waiting for news of the unknown may be more dreadful than experiencing the actualities. So all America suffered with us. So all America is responding for our relief. So all America will rejoice in our recovery.

Joining in the spirit of optimism in the face of catastrophe the *Miami Herald* published the following editorial on Wednesday:

THE REAL MIAMI SPIRIT

Every Miamian has a right to be proud of his city and proud of her people.

It is characteristic of the American people that they take disaster with a courageous spirit. Trouble evaporates among them when they face conditions, and they heroically turn to the rehabilitation necessary after destruction of homes and property.

So with Miami. Five days have elapsed since a hurricane of unprecedented proportions visited the city, carrying with it destruction to many homes, injuries to thousands of others, rendering many families homeless and temporarily without shelter, food or raiment.

But has anybody complained at misfortune? No! Emphatically, no! Every one of those who have lost through the storm has courageously taken up the burden and is pushing on with a cheerful fortitude that marks our people as being peculiarly brave and determined. That is the true Miami spirit, brought out most strongly in time of distress.

We talked about the Miami spirit when everything was moving along smoothly, when every one was prosperous and happy. But that was not the real Miami spirit. That has been displayed to perfection within the past few days.

A cheerful determination to make the best of things, a ready helpfulness to assist the less fortunate, a wonderful spirit of cooperation—these are the true indications of the Miami spirit, and they have been shown in a remarkable degree.

So, after all, we have much to be thankful for. And we may go forward with full confidence that the spirit that has characterized the people of Miami within the past week will yet, and very speedily, build a very much greater and better Miami.

Never can we forget, nor can the world forget, that the people of Miami, imbued with the real Miami spirit, in the midst of serious disaster, did not lose

courage, that they did not repine at misfortune, that they turned toward the future with confidence in the final greatness of their beloved city.

We have all been knit more closely together by having together experienced serious trouble.

The following official statement was issued on Tuesday, following the storm, by George E. Merrick, founder of Coral Gables, and his official associates:

"A careful survey just completed by the City of Coral Gables and the Coral Gables Corporation and the Chamber of Commerce of the City of Coral Gables reveals that the hurricane, which visited this section of Florida last Saturday did less damage in the City of Coral Gables than in any other sections of the Greater Miami district. One reason for this is that all buildings in Coral Gables are of concrete or tile construction, which was better able to withstand the force of the storm than frame construction. Practically all of the roofs of the houses in Coral Gables are of tile and on a number of houses some of this roofing tile was dislodged by the force of the gale, but such damage is easily repaired by replacing the tile at a cost which is not great. Almost every house in Coral Gables had brightly colored awnings and for the most part these awnings were destroyed and the awning frames broke a number of windows, which caused some damage from rain, but again this damage is of a superficial nature and can be easily repaired by the replacing of the broken glass and the placing of new awnings, which are frequently renewed from time to time in any event. Some few buildings of lighter construction were blown down and a few roofs were blown off and others were partially damaged, but on the whole the damage to roofs can be repaired within a very short time at not extensive cost.

"Considerable temporary damage was done to the trees and shrubs throughout Coral Gables, large numbers of which were blown down by the storm, but the very nature of our tropical growth and tropical soil is such that the immediate replanting and setting up of these trees and shrubs in their former location will result in the saving of practically all of them. Great care is being given this landscape work; large forces of men began the restoration of this planting within a few hours after the storm passed. Within one month's time it is believed that all traces of the storm in Coral Gables will have been entirely removed.

"The utility plants owned and operated by the Florida Power & Light Company, a subsidiary of the American

Power & Light Company and the Electric Bond and Share Company of New York, were damaged by the blowing down of poles and wires in the electric distribution system and by the destruction of one of the system of five water towers. Within two hours after the storm subsided water service was restored to practically all parts of Coral Gables and within about 30 hours, electric light current was made available to the Tallman Hospital in Coral Gables, and on the second day after the storm, is being rapidly extended to other important buildings.

"The Miami-Biltmore Hotel, which is the finest structure in Coral Gables, having a plant valued at ten million dollars, escaped with very little damage and such damage as it did receive was entirely covered by tornado insurance. The Antilla, San Sebastian, Casa Loma and Cla-Reina Hotels, and the Coral Gables Inn were also very little damaged, and this was very fortunate because these hotels were enabled to house and furnish food for not only such residents of Coral Gables whose homes were temporarily damaged by water, but also to a number of people from districts outside of Coral Gables, whose frame homes were in many cases entirely destroyed by the storm.

"A conservative estimate of the total damage of every nature in the City of Coral Gables, made from figures carefully compiled as a result of the citywide survey, will not exceed one and one-half million dollars, and happily about one-third of this sum is covered by tornado insurance, and the remainder is so well distributed between the City of Coral Gables, the Coral Gables Corporation and individual property owners, that it will not fall as any great burden upon any particular class, although of course there are individual cases which require assistance.

"The people of Coral Gables have shown a splendid spirit of unselfishness, cheerfulness and helpfulness, at this time. A splendidly efficient organization was formed within a few hours after the storm passed to handle the work of immediate repair of such damage as was done and to control the proper distribution of food supplies until normal conditions were restored. So well was this work done, that within 36 hours all restrictions as to food supplies were withdrawn. Fortunately, there is sufficient food in the Greater Miami district to abundantly supply all needs for a period of 30 days, even though none additional were received, and since railroad communication was restored within 24 hours, no danger exists from this source, nor is any outside assistance in food supplies required at this time.

"By reason of the fact that the water system in Coral Gables was reopened within two hours after the storm, sanitary conditions have been excellent and no anxiety need be felt for the city, which is under the supervision of a splendidly organized and equipped health department. No disorder of any nature has arisen. The excellent work of the city's police department has protected the property and safety of the city.

"Splendid service has been rendered the people of outlying districts at the Tallman Hospital in Coral Gables, by reason of the fact that they sustained less damage than in some other sections, have been enabled to furnish homes and assistance to persons who were less fortunate. No deaths whatever have been reported of people of the City of Coral Gables. The damage done by the hurricane in other parts of the Greater Miami district, as well as in Coral Gables, has been greatly exaggerated, and it is proper that a correct and authorized statement of this damage should be furnished to the people of America so that no erroneous impression will be created. There will be no change in the future plans of Coral Gables. The University of Miami is scheduled to open in Coral Gables on the 15th day of October, 1926. In the absence of any unforeseen circumstances, the occurrence of which does not now seem at all probable, the University of Miami will open on schedule time, and from present indications, the enrollment will exceed 600 in number.

"The rapid transit railway, temporarily disabled through damage to the trolley system, will be restored in the near future and its operation extended to Sunset Road as planned. In the meantime, Coral Gables busses are operating to and from Miami over the rapid transit route and throughout the residential district of Coral Gables.

"Coral Gables and Miami expect and will have many visitors within the next few months. So rapidly are repairs being made in the entire district that it is certain that Greater Miami, including the City of Coral Gables, will be ready to adequately care for all of its visitors this winter.

"This official statement has been prepared under the auspices of and its accuracy is attested by George E. Merrick, President of the Coral Gables Corporation, and builder of the City of Coral Gables; Telfair Knight, General Manager of the Coral Gables Corporation; Edward E. Dammers, Mayor of the City of Coral Gables; F. J. O'Leary, President of the Chamber of Commerce, Rodney S. Miller, in charge of reconstruction work; and M. P. Lehman, Director of Public Safety of the City of Coral Gables."

Carl G. Fisher, pioneer developer of Miami Beach, is among the first to begin rehabilitation. The *Miami Daily News* of Friday says the following about Mr. Fisher:

WORDS OF CHEER.

From Carl G. Fisher, pioneer Miami Beach developer, comes the word that the order to rebuild supersedes all others.

From John McEntee Bowman comes the message that the hurricane has done no permanent damage to this city or its suburbs; that out of the ruins of the old will arise a bigger and stronger city that will attract tourists as never before.

From scores of lesser men come messages of hope and promises of assistance.

These are the words which hearten those of us who passed through the storm, saw it at its worst and emerged from it determined to carry on.

If words can add to the courage of Miamians, then all fear of a pessimistic reaction is dissipated.

Millions of dollars in insurance losses will be paid in this area. This money will go back into new buildings and repairs. This means work and plenty of it for labor. It means increased activity among retailers who will supply the daily wants of the community and the demand will be felt by the wholesaler and producer.

Already hundreds of permits have been issued for repair work. The song of hammer and saw has replaced the roar of the gale.

We are at work rebuilding our city and words of cheer from acknowledged leaders of industry, who are financially interested in this city and its progress, will speed us to our objective.

Prediction of what the coming three months will bring in reconstruction is contained in the following editorial from the *Miami Herald* of Friday:

NINETY DAYS HENCE.

Anyone who comes at all in contact with the people of Miami in these days and retains any spirit of gloom must be a hopeless pessimist. It is a naturally depressing thing to see the widespread property damage wrought by the hurricane, and to know of the suffering caused to so many of the people. But the depression is wonderfully lightened when one comes in touch with the splendid spirit of real optimism, the unselfishness, the feeling of brotherliness, that permeates the very atmosphere.

The next two or three weeks will be a real testing time. During the past few days there has been the sustaining force of excitement. This will pass and there will be a time of grim toil and sacrifice. Miami will go through this with the same courage that has been shown already. The fine spirit that is seen everywhere gives assurance of this. Aid is coming from the whole nation. This will help keep up morale.

Miami has met the situation so far as probably no other city ever has in a time of disaster. Those who have been in other places in similar times are a unit in declaring that the city has been organized to meet the crisis in a really wonderful way.

The streets of the down-town section are cleared. There are few indications of a storm. Business is proceeding. Everybody is busy and cheerful. Houses are being repaired. The people are planning to adjust themselves to the unusual conditions.

Within a month most of the visible signs of the hurricane will have disappeared. Within three months Miami will be ready to receive its visitors and make them welcome. There will be nothing to prevent giving the thousands who will come the same comfortable and pleasant treatment that they have always received. By January 1 we will have ceased to think or talk of the hurricane. It will have written its story in the history of the city, but Miami will be looking forward, not backward.

Official report of Weather Bureau of Barometer Readings which show the lowest reading ever recorded in the United States. Figures given by R. W. Gray, United States Government Meteorologist, Miami, Fla.:

At 10 p. m. of September 17th, 1926, the barometer began to fall rapidly from 29.20 inches, and at midnight it had fallen .11 inch. From midnight to 6.45 a. m., at which time the center of the storm passed over Miami, there was a precipitate fall at the rate of .28 inch per hour. From about 5.30 a. m. to 6.10 a. m., the barometer fell .40 inch and then remained stationary for 15 or 20 minutes. This was at the beginning of the lull in the wind which attended the arrival of the center of the storm. After the short stationary period, there was another rapid fall of .06 inch, and at 6.45 a. m., a reading of the mercurial barometer showed a pressure of 27.61 inches. The barograph pen fell to 27.54 inches. The master of the steamship Crudeoil, one of the few vessels that rode out the storm in Biscayne Bay, had his aneroid barometer adjusted at this office the day preceding the storm. His instrument recorded 27.59

inches. This reading required a correction of .01 inch to reduce it to sea level, so that the corrected reading is 27.60 inches. After the center of the storm had passed over the barometer rose rapidly and at noon, September 18th, stood at 29.30 inches.

Official Record of Wind Velocity attained during storm of September 17-18, 1926, as reported and given by B. C. Kadel, United States Weather Bureau, Washington, D. C.

TRUE VELOCITY OF STORM WIND WAS
132 MILES.

Washington report shows highest ever recorded in the United States.

Official recognition of the wind velocity at Miami Beach during the September hurricane, as the highest ever recorded by automatic instruments in the United States, is given in a statement issued by Benjamin C. Kadel, chief of the instrument division of the United States Weather Bureau at Washington, D. C., just received by Richard W. Gray, government meteorologist at Miami.

Corrected to show true velocity, the readings of the anenometer at Allison hospital show an extreme of 132 miles an hour for a two-minute period between 7 and 8 a. m., September 18, while it is impossible to determine the extreme true velocity for any single mile of wind from the record, Mr. Kadel's statement shows. During the two minutes for which the extreme true velocity of 132 miles an hour was recorded, five miles of wind passed the instrument.

The extreme true velocity of 132 miles an hour, the weather bureau's instrument chief finds, corresponds to 57 pounds of pressure per square foot on a flat surface "normal to the wind."

The highest true velocity previously recorded was 140 miles an hour at Mt. Washington, N. H., on January 11, 1876, for one mile of wind. Mr. Kadel does not attempt to fix the extreme velocity for one mile of wind at Miami Beach, but says that it would exceed this record at Mt. Washington.

Mr. Gray believes if the extreme velocity for one mile of wind at Allison hospital could be determined accurately, it would show approximately 150 miles an hour.

The instrument at Allison hospital is a three-cup anenometer, regarded as much more accurate than the common four-cup type by the weather bureau. Had the same wind been measured on the four-cup type of anenometer, 183 miles an hour would have been shown as the extreme velocity, while the three-cup instrument registeerd 138 miles an hour, a variance of but six degrees from the true velocity.

Rise of the water that resulted from this hurricane also was the greatest ever caused by a storm on the coast of the United States, Mr. Gray reports. The ocean rose 11.7 feet above mean sea level in Biscayne boulevard, his records show, while a higher rise, estimated at from 14 to 15 feet, occurred in the Coconut Grove district.

Official Report of Red Cross on October 9th, 1926, regarding relief given, deaths, injuries and families affected in affected area of hurricane of September 17-18, 1926:

For the period, September 20th to noon, October 9th, Red Cross relief had been given as follows, the figures being for the entire storm-stricken area: Food to 6,500; clothing to 4,650; medical and nursing service to 113,200; building and repair jobs to houses to 12,330; tents to accommodate 11,900.

The following is a summary of storm damage, with the exception of property damage, as compiled by Red Cross dated October 9th, for all places in Florida damaged by the hurricane of September 17-18, 1926:

ESTIMATES OF STORM DAMAGE.

Area.	Dead.	Injured.	Families Affected.
Fort Lauderdale	17	1,800	4,800
Pompano	..	.....	250
Davie	2	6	85
Hollywood	39	750	1,500
Fort Myers	2	3	149
Moore Haven	150	50	600
Hialeah	26	800	1,500
Miami	115	1,300	5,000
Miami Beach	17	1,632	2,000
Rural Dade County	5	40	2,000
Total	373	6,381	17,884

These figures were furnished by Mr. Baker, who is in charge of Red Cross relief in the stricken area.

NOTE.—These figures do not include relief given by American Legion, Elks, Masons, K. of C., K. K. K., and other fraternal relief committees, who did wonderful work and service to the people in the entire stricken area, and who took charge of many cases, which were not reported to the Red Cross.

Mayor Romfh reminds Miami's citizens of their duty to the Deity:

A CALL FOR THANKSGIVING

To All of the People of Miami:

Your city, the one you have loved so well, has suffered a temporary disaster almost beyond comprehension, but much, very much, remains upon which to build for the future. Loss of property has been great, but that loss will be much mitigated; loss of lives, fortunately, has been much less than first reported; the great majority have our loved ones with us and safe; we have all of our courage, determination and optimism.

Now, Therefore, I, Edward Coleman Romfh, mayor of the city of Miami, do hereby call upon the people of Miami to assemble in their respective houses of worship on next Sunday and there offer up sincere thanksgiving to Almighty God for His help in time of need and His protection from great dangers, for health and strength and courage.

For those who have no regular church connection continuous religious services will be provided from 11 a. m. to 1 p. m. on Sunday at Royal Palm Park, and all of our people are earnestly requested to attend them.

E. C. ROMFH, *Mayor.*

A summing up of the disaster was made by Mayor E. C. Romfh on Saturday, September 25th, one week after the hurricane. Mayor Romfh's statement deals only with Dade County and takes no account of the storm's ravages at Hollywood, Dania, Fort Lauderdale, Homestead or Moore Haven. His statement follows:

"From the thousands of telegrams pouring into Miami, hundreds of which are addressed to the mayor of the city, I am convinced a very much exaggerated idea of Miami's real condition has been created. I regard it as a duty to the public at large to set forth as briefly as possible the situation as it now exists and its relation to the future of this city.

"The West Indian hurricane which swept over an area of 60 miles on the Atlantic coast on September 18, extending 30 miles north and 30 miles south of Miami, was by far the most severe and destructive storm that ever touched the mainland of the United States. Miami in her 30 years of existence has never been materially damaged before.

"There was a great amount of damage to buildings through their unroofing, the breaking of windows and the blowing down of poorly constructed buildings in the outlying districts. The larger business buildings, the better constructed homes, hotels and apartments were mostly damaged by the breaking of glass and in some instances the covering of roofs were loosened or blown off and thus the heavy rain created the most damage. There was great destruction to the tropical palms and foliage.

"The electric light plant, water and gas systems were put out of commission. The water and gas service now is normal. The electric system has been restored in the central business district and service to large residential areas is being added daily.

"The most regrettable part of the storm was the number of deaths which totals 106 to date in Dade county. There were 854 injured placed in regular and temporary hospitals, 450 of whom have been discharged. The citizens committee did heroic work the first few days in caring for the injured. However, this work has now been taken over by the Red Cross and this organization is handling the situation with the utmost efficiency.

"Small buildings in outlying districts, cheaply constructed, were blown down. It was in these and in houseboats that the greatest number of deaths occurred. There was great damage done to yachts and pleasure boats, but most of these will be put in shipshape order for the coming season.

"Of the 150 hotels in Miami, Miami Beach and Coral

E. C. ROMFH, Mayor of Miami
President of the First National Bank of Miami

Gables, 75 per cent were not damaged to any great extent. The year around hotels are operating as usual. Of the 1,200 apartment houses, 70 per cent received little damage. All hotels and apartment houses will be completely repaired and put in first-class condition within 60 days.

"There are thousands who have lost all and are destitute and who must have financial aid in order to get back upon a self-supporting basis. There are the smaller home owners, smaller tradesmen, workers and people of very moderate means. It is to aid these people that the citizens' relief committee and the Red Cross issue their appeal for assistance. That need is acute and genuine.

"But there are other thousands who have the finances or can make satisfactory arrangements to restore their own homes and replace effects damaged or destroyed. These are contributing to the aid of their destitute neighbors, but financing their own losses makes it impossible for them to contribute in sufficient amounts to supply all the urgent needs. Miami greatly appreciates the spontaneous sympathy which has been shown by the American people as expressed by President Coolidge.

"In the six days that have passed since the storm, this city has come back with a speed that is absolutely amazing. No one who has not been on the ground, checking up the progress, can realize the tremendous recovery, a united, courageous, indefatigable citizenship has made.

"Day and night, with little sleep, tens of thousands of men and women have cooperatively labored, not only to relieve the suffering, to feed the hungry, to house the homeless, but to repair, to rebuild and to remove the debris left in the wake of the storm.

"I want to give positive assurance that our friends will find Miami this winter the same enjoyable, hospitable, comfortable vacation city it has always been.

"I predict that Miami will make a world come-back. The people here have the enthusiasm, the will to do, an unshakable faith in the future of this great city. It is the same people who have created the fastest growing city in America who are now turning their energies and enthusiasm to the work of reconstruction in Miami.

(Signed) "CITY OF MIAMI,
"E. C. ROMFH, Mayor."